JAPAN'S WAR MEMORIES

This book is dedicated to Ienaga Saburo and his supporters who have devoted their lives to the struggle for truth in Japanese textbooks. Ienaga was born in 1913, and his life since 1965 has been dedicated to the legal struggle to tell the truth especially about Japan's role in the war. His is the inspiration behind almost every page in this book. Without Ienaga this book would lack much of its focus. At the time of writing (22 December 1996) we are still waiting for the final Supreme Court decision, but whatever the final outcome, there is no doubt that Ienaga's life has not been lived in vain: Japanese textbooks are now more truthful.

Japan's War Memories

Amnesia or concealment?

GEORGE HICKS

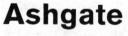

Aldershot • Brookfield USA • Singapore • Sydney

Published by
Ashgate Publishing Limited
Gower House
Croft Road
Aldershot
Hants GU11 3HR
England

Ashgate Publishing Company
Old Post Road
Brookfield
Vermont 05036
USA

British Library Cataloguing in Publication Data

Hicks, George
     Japan's war memories : amnesia or concealment?
     1. Atrocities - Japan 2. World War, 1939-1945 - Japan -
     Atrocities 3. Japan - History - 1926-1945 4. Japan - History
     - 1945- 5. Japan - Politics and government - 1945-
     I. Title
     952' .033

Library of Congress Catalog Card Number: 97-73875

ISBN 1 84014 164 6

Printed and bound by Athenaeum Press, Ltd.,
Gateshead, Tyne & Wear.

Contents

Acknowledgments

Every author depends on the help of others, but in my case the role played by Ms Yumi Lee, Ms Kawashima Megumi, and Les Oates is quite exceptional. Together we have written three books on relatively unknown aspects of Japanese imperialism: *The Comfort Women* (1995), the story of the Korean minority in Japan, *Japan's Hidden Apartheid* (1997) and now *Japan's War Memories* (1997). Yumi is a third generation Korean Japanese who supplied the bulk of the written sources for all three books. Megumi also supplied a lot of material including the invaluable *Textbook Suit News* which kept us up to date on the legal aspects of the textbook cases. Les is a retired senior lecturer in Japanese and a translator and writer of exceptional talent. This project has absorbed much of our life over the last five years, and there is no adequate way I can say 'thank you.'

Introduction

After tracking Nazi war criminals for 17 years, the United States Justice Department took its first action on 3 December 1996 against Japanese army veterans suspected of medically experimenting on prisoners and operating forced sex camps during the Second World War. Sixteen men who served in the Imperial Army were barred from ever entering the United States.

These were the first Japanese placed on the U.S. government's 'watch list' since it was established in 1979 to exclude people who engaged in persecution on behalf of Nazi Germany or its allies. More than 60,000 people have been put on the list since 1979, but these are the first Japanese.

Although this is a study of Japanese wartime 'amnesia,' it is obvious from the above example that American amnesia towards Japanese war criminals is staggering, though some reasons for this are advanced in this book. The Nanking massacre is another war atrocity about which new material is only just emerging. A rare war diary was made public for the first time on 12 December 1996. The diary of businessman John Rabe has only just been released with the permission of Mr Rabe's 80-year-old son Otto. Running to 2,117 pages, it contains hitherto unknown eyewitness accounts of Japanese atrocities during the siege of Nanking in 1937. Japanese scholars of various political hues are well aware that first, much research remains to be done on most aspects of the war and secondly, what is known is poorly disseminated.

An advocate of right wing revisionist views on Japan's role in the Asia-Pacific War, many of whose views are certainly open to question, at least showed some insight in claiming that 'the Greater East Asia War [the right wing's term] is a treasure house [of data] for the study of the Japanese.' His argument runs:

> The German General Staff, after being defeated in the First World War, conducted thorough research into that war.... But in Japan scarcely any research is being pursued on the Greater East Asia War, not only in the field of strategy and tactics, but also into organization and structure

and the characteristics of the Japanese people and armed forces, even though it is a treasure house packed with all kinds of relevant data. (Komuro et al. 1995)

Although as this book demonstrates, a massive quantity of mainly narrative material on the war has been published, this generally lacks much analytical or critical content. On the other hand, while there has also been a great deal of debate on the war, especially since related issues were resurrected as the smoke screen of the Cold War faded, such debate has been highly colored by ideological biases of many kinds.

Komuro Naoki (quoted above) reflects something of the more radical stream in the right wing, which has always been critical of the Japanese establishment, sometimes to the point of violence. So although defending or mitigating Japan's wartime role in some respects, he also condemns much of the manner in which the establishment both precipitated the war and conducted it. During the war itself the radical right were so dissatisfied with the current regime that some even plotted the assassination of Prime Minister General Tojo while others successfully contested the 1942 wartime election in opposition to the officially sponsored list of candidates.

There were two main reasons for this. First, the radical right had advocated social reorganization along state socialist lines under the Emperor to prepare for war against the dominant Western powers, whereas in fact the Zaibatsu combines retained a leading role in the wartime economy. Secondly, as Tojo himself had combined the roles of Prime Minister, War Minister, and Home Minister, with some other temporary ministerial roles, he was seen as recreating the dictatorial role of the Shoguns of feudal times, who are condemned in the right wing ideology as usurping the supremacy that properly belongs to the Emperor alone. The most extreme accused Tojo of being a crypto-Communist who had led Japan into an exhausting war as a means of precipitating social revolution.

Debate on the war only became prominent, particularly on the international scene, after the decline of the Cold War order. Until then, as Japan had been the only clearly viable Asian ally of the Western camp in the confrontation with Communism, the Second World War tended to be treated as a dead issue. This was clearly indicated by the Western camp's relinquishment of reparation claims in the Peace Treaty, in the interests of Japan's revival as a much needed ally. The majority of Japanese, especially the restored establishment, were of course happy to accept this situation. Asian countries, on the other hand, were either under Communist rule, threatened by insurgency, or dependent on Japanese economic aid, so were not in a position to pursue issues affecting them which had resulted from the war.

This made it possible for Japanese official and business circles to avoid reference to the war to an extent that, to foreign observers especially, seemed to amount to a kind of 'national amnesia.' Contexts where this was especially noted were the omission or minimization of references to the war in historical education and the very limited nature of any official commemoration of the war, either in the form of memorials or the observance of War Dead Commemoration Day on 15 August. This event, attended by the heads of government, was before 1993 purely an occasion of mourning rather than any reflection on the nature of the war. The press too tended to avoid war-related topics, so that the reading public's picture of the war was mainly derived from published memoir type material, sometimes semifictionalized. As mentioned, however, this has been so voluminous as to cast some doubt on how far such apparent official 'amnesia' affects the population as a whole. Psychologically, of course, the very strong taboo in Japanese society on matters likely to cause embarrassment is a factor on a more personal level.

It was only from the early 1980s that the decay of Cold War alignments allowed the open revival, after so long, of war-related issues. The first conspicuous case was the Asia-wide uproar in 1982 over the distortion of Japan's wartime role in its school textbooks. This was followed over succeeding years by steadily expanding demands for compensation and apology, mainly among Asians but also including some Western claimants on an individual basis. This is one reason why such issues are much alive at present in the context of Japan's relations with Asian countries, who demand some definitive resolution of the kind that, but for the Cold War, might have been made decades ago.

Within Japan itself, however, the question of war guilt or responsibility had always been a matter of concern among left wing and pacifist groups in their efforts to block moves to revise the postwar Constitution, especially Article 9. This reads:

> 1. Aspiring sincerely to an international peace based on justice and order, the Japanese people forever renounce war as a sovereign right of the nation and the threat or use of force as a means of settling international disputes.
> 2. In order to accomplish the aim of the preceding paragraph, land, sea and air forces, as well as other war potential, will never be maintained. The right of belligerency of the state will not be recognized.

The application of this article has been weakened to some extent by Supreme Court rulings that purely defensive armament does not infringe it. Then, following the Gulf War in 1991, the then dominant Liberal Democratic party, under U.S. pressure, had the Diet pass legislation enabling the dispatch overseas of forces participating in United Nations peacekeeping operations. Some establishment and right wing elements have, however, been pressing for constitutional revision allowing unrestricted rearmament and some strengthening of the Emperor's role, which has been reduced to one of national symbol rather than sovereign.

The motivation of the left wing and its sympathizers in opposing such moves includes memories of their own savage suppression under the wartime regime and also extends to resentment of the 'reverse course' in occupation policies in the interests of Cold War strategy. This had reversed the initial purge of the wartime leadership (equivalent to the more permanent denazification in Germany) and encouraged rearmament on a generally reluctant nation. Constitutional revision requires a two-thirds vote by both houses of the Diet and a referendum and, as the left wing parties, with the Buddhist Komeito party, have between them always gained over one-third of Lower House seats, the long dominant LDP was unable to initiate the process. A committee to make recommendations for this functioned for a time around 1960, but the issue was not pressed and some elements in the highly factionalized LDP were far from enthusiastic, as the status quo was proving so beneficial to Japan, politically and economically.

During that period, however, controls over the content of education materials also developed reactionary tendencies, largely under pressure from the conservative wing of the LDP, probably with a view to conditioning the public mind for ultimate constitutional revision. This in turn was resolutely countered by opposing elements, particularly strong in the teaching and other professions. From 1965, this action has taken the form of substantial litigation at all levels of the judiciary, centered on the heroic figure of Professor Ienaga Saburo, aimed at freeing education from authoritarian controls and more specifically to expose the nature of former Japanese militarism as a means of discouraging constitutional revision.

This combination of both internal and international revival of wartime issues has stimulated a considerable backlash among conservative nationalist elements, generally classed as right wing revisionists, who among other motives sometimes show a sense of betrayal by the West on the earlier assumption that if Japan played its part in the Cold War, as it did, earlier offenses would be forgiven. Views and arguments within this camp do vary considerably and range from bald denials that some notorious episodes even occurred to more sophisticated treatment of some debatable issues. All, however, would favor constitutional revision in some form, and with a new electoral system, the opposition may not always be able to maintain its blocking power in the Diet. Various proposals for revision are being debated and from this viewpoint too the questions raised in this book are very much alive.

Apart from tactical considerations on both the internal and the international fronts, more abstract questions of war guilt or responsibility are often raised. The official policy of the Western allies, in the interests of Cold War solidarity, was to treat the question of war guilt as settled by the Tokyo trials which, though in a sense passing judgment on Japan, narrowed actual blame to a small sample of the very complex ruling elites. Many Japanese as well as others have felt that this approach was inadequate. The trials themselves were so arbitrarily selective and dominated by immediate political considerations that they are hardly satisfactory on the legal or philosophical level.

More broadly, the definition of guilt itself can be problematic. Insofar as guilt is usually defined as arising from a moral choice, it is difficult to apportion it clearly to the vast majority of Japanese who were excluded from any decision-making role by the military-dominated totalitarian regime that precipitated the war. Some, however, like Professor Ienaga, have expressed a feeling of guilt for not having tried to oppose the regime, though the fate of some who did demonstrates that this required exceptional heroism and independence of mind.

It is still more problematic, of course, to apportion guilt to the vast majority of the present population born since the war. It is probably sounder to describe these as having inherited not so much a guilt involving a choice, but a legal type corporate responsibility, in so far as a nation is a continuing corporate entity. Professor Ienaga speaks of a 'negative inheritance' or 'inherited debt.' This is a theme that has been raised in some other countries in the context of claims by indigenous peoples who fell victim in the period of Western expansionism. Some Japanese nationalist apologists have sought to counter the concept of a peculiarly Japanese guilt by portraying Japan as simply one contestant in the struggle between rival imperialisms, to which a critic replies: 'It is true that Japanese imperialism arose within the framework of Western aggression in Asia but if this is used to justify Japanese aggression it becomes impossible to condemn the evils committed by Western forces during their own ascendancy.' (Shida 1989)

A writer cited in this book, who in the 1970s led the effort to expose the Japanese army's record in China, speaks of himself as not feeling an individual responsibility for the war, having then been a child, but takes the position: 'Simply to "apologize" for the militarism of the past does not serve any real purpose. The real apology would lie in averting the present threat of militarization.' (Honda 1983)

This, at least, has practical relevance in the current situation.

" negative inheritance "

xi

1 Under the occupation and 'reverse course' (1945-1952)

As is generally known, Japan's part in the Second World War was terminated by the Emperor's action, contrary to precedent, in the Supreme Council for the Direction of the War. Up to that time he had refrained from any initiative to end the war. The reason he habitually gave was that, as a constitutional monarch under the 1889 Constitution, he was obliged to accept the advice of the government and, in operational matters, the politically independent supreme command of the armed forces; his relation to the latter being that of titular commander-in-chief. Some authorities also emphasize a retiring temperament as a factor, perhaps as a result of the very peculiar upbringing unavoidable in his 'transcendent' role.

It was only when the Council was evenly divided on whether to continue the war, following the atomic bomb attacks and the subsequent Soviet entry into the war, that he was able, after some complex discussion with personal advisors, to exercise a casting vote, as it were, for surrender. The last sticking point holding up acceptance of the Allies' Potsdam Declaration, calling for unconditional surrender, was concern for the fate of the Imperial House as the fulcrum of Japan's national identity. The government's preparedness to accept the declaration was cabled to the U.S. Secretary of State, with the sole reservation that 'the said declaration does not comprise any demand which prejudices the prerogatives of his Majesty as a Sovereign Ruler.'

The U.S. reply included the statement that 'the ultimate form of government in Japan shall be established by the freely expressed will of the Japanese people.' The Japanese Minister to Sweden, through which peace feelers had been extended for some time earlier, advised that the reply was being interpreted internationally as implying noninterference with the Emperor system, upon which the declaration was accepted.

Even after this decision, army diehards unsuccessfully invaded the palace in an attempt to prevent the Emperor's surrender rescript from being broadcast, on the theory that he had been misled by disloyal advisors—an episode which is sometimes quoted to demonstrate that at any earlier stage a surrender

1

could not have been smoothly carried through. The mass of the people were, of course, quite unprepared for the announcement, having received only highly censored news and been for some time conditioned to prepare for 'the decisive battle for the homeland,' designed to inflict heavy enough casualties on the invading allies to obtain a peace settlement on terms short of unconditional surrender.

In order to brief the media on the required manner of presenting this devastating development, the head of the Cabinet Information Bureau, which had been in control of censorship, held a meeting of representatives on the day before the broadcast. This 'unprecedented national disaster' was to be presented in the terms that the nation as a whole was to share responsibility for it and to apologize profoundly to the Sovereign. 'Any Communist or socialistic form of expression arising amid the confusion of defeat is to be sternly suppressed. Criticism of the armed forces and government leadership is strictly forbidden.' (Irokawa 1995)

The possibility of a Marxist revolution in the event of defeat, as had happened in a number of other countries, had been a nightmare among the establishment since at least early in 1945. Since February, Prince Konoe, one of the most prominent civil politicians, had been advising the Emperor to end the war to forestall social breakdown and revolution. This possibility was probably undermined, at least in part, by the Soviet attack in the last week of the war, widely condemned as opportunistic and treacherous in view of the Neutrality Pact concluded with Japan early in 1941.

For the moment, the press, if only through inertia, could not easily depart from the information chief's instructions. The *Asahi,* once the stronghold of liberal journalism from the 19th century origins of the party movement until the imposition of wartime controls and later to resume this role, supplemented factual reporting with an editorial which did not yet break with wartime ideology:

> The spirit of the Greater East Asian declaration [following the declaration of war] aiming at the liberation of oppressed peoples [in the Western colonial empires] and the reconstruction of national states free of exploitation and servitude, together with the display of the Special Attack [*kamikaze*] spirit unique to our forces, may be described as honorable achievements in the course of the Greater East Asia War and these, irrespective of the outcome of the war, must be regarded as the fair fruit of our national character, to be recorded forever. (Ishida 1995)

But only a few days later the question of war responsibility, now seen as something highly negative, began to be raised in another *Asahi* editorial:

> Responsibility is not by any means to be attributed only to a particular set of people but borne by all hundred million of our nation, yet at

2

the same time there are varying degrees of responsibility. The responsibility of the media in particular must be admitted to be extremely heavy. Even if, from the standpoint of the present, it may be claimed that there was no other course for us to take, we must humbly reflect on whether there was not some other recourse in our mode of proceeding. On the one hand being actually aware of our past responsibility and anxious to atone for it, we on the other hand steadfastly hope for a healthy development of the media in the future. (Ishida 1995)

Other newspapers followed a similar course, and there was considerable replacement of senior staff identified with wartime policies, but meanwhile, only ten days into September, a new type of control in the form of occupation censorship came to be raised. A memorandum was addressed by occupation General Headquarters to the Japanese government, which was being left in place as the instrument of allied control, regarding the 'freedom of press and media.' It comprised the following points:

1. Prohibition of false reports or any threatening public security.
2. Restrictions on freedom of expression to be kept to a minimum and debate on Japan's future to be encouraged so long as it does not impede Japan's efforts to join the comity of peace-loving nations.
3. Prohibition of discussion on the activities of the [occupation] forces, other than official announcements, and of false or subversive criticism or rumors regarding allied countries.
4. Broadcast news or commentary for the present to be restricted to Tokyo Broadcasting Station; others to be confined to entertainment.
5. Publications or broadcasting stations making false reports or any threatening public security will be suspended or closed.

The implementation of these policies inevitably involved complexities and inconsistencies and gradually increased in scope and severity, but these developments are best left until later. The allies had also considered the possibility of a revolt against the established order and instructions to the Supreme Commander, General MacArthur, had even indicated that, if such a movement arose the occupation should not suppress it. The reasoning was that reform on Japanese initiative would be more durable than any imposed from outside, but MacArthur and more senior staff were wary of any such movement getting out of control, especially if it took a Marxist direction. This concern deepened as the Cold War intensified and little scope was allowed for Japanese initiative.

On the political level, the cabinet that had presided over the war's last phases was replaced by one headed by Prince Higashikuni Naruhiko, a member of the imperial clan and husband of an aunt of the Emperor. He was an army general of some prominence who had had a long career including postings in Europe and service on the Asian continent, and had also developed a

3

wider political network among the establishment than any other member of the imperial clan (the Emperor himself of course being insulated from political maneuvers outside his institutional roles). He had more than once been considered a prime ministerial candidate in the early years when the acute factional struggles and spectacular terrorism leading up to the war had seemed to need an imperial head of government to avert breakdown in the political process. In later 1941 in particular, when the last cabinet before Pearl Harbor, headed by Prince Konoe (a court noble), resigned on reaching a deadlock in negotiations with the United States, the then War Minister Tojo, who regarded war as inevitable, proposed Higashikuni as Prime Minister a means of ensuring national solidarity in that event.

The Emperor, however, typically cautious, took the view that the Imperial House itself would be jeopardized if one of its members headed a government that initiated war. This implied that, if the war were lost, the Imperial House could not evade responsibility for it and would face the fate of the German and Russian monarchies after the First World War. So Tojo was appointed, not because of any charisma but because his career had been so closely linked to the military police (Kempeitai) that these were virtually his personal henchmen and could be entrusted to enforce national solidarity by their own notorious means. For some time they had been extending their normal role of keeping order in the army to one of general suppression of dissidence in the name of national security.

But now, in the ultimate emergency of defeat, Higashikuni was the logical candidate to inherit the task of achieving a smooth transition to peace. He could now use the prestige of the Imperial House for this purpose and, being an army general, could exercise the force of military discipline as distinct from civil authority. Most importantly, though, from the Emperor's point of view, he would if successful demonstrate to the allies the need to maintain the role of the Imperial House as a guarantee of social stability, even if, as was sometimes contemplated, the Emperor himself should abdicate. The establishment was already aware of the approach of the Cold War and hoped to turn it to Japan's advantage. In the farewell address by the Chief of the Naval Staff to his subordinates, he urged them to cooperate with the Occupation because the United States would soon be at war with the Soviet Union and Japan could make a comeback as America's ally. It was through such reasoning that ultranationalist elements, who had been expected to cause the occupation the most trouble, turned out to be a negligible problem in contrast to those presented, in the occupation's view, by left wing or radical reformist elements or 'liberated' Koreans.

Prince Higashikuni fulfilled his role successfully in all respects and General MacArthur's personal contacts with the Emperor seem to have confirmed to him the need to retain the Emperor system to avoid social destabilization and to spare the Emperor himself any attribution of war guilt, even to the limited extent requiring abdication. In Prime Minister Higashikuni's first press conference, intended to direct the public mind along the required lines, he stated:

> This situation has of course come about partly because government policies were wrong but another factor was the decline in moral principles among the nation. On this occasion I believe that the whole nation—armed forces, officials, and people, must engage in thorough self-criticism and repent. I believe that general penitence by the whole nation is the first step in the reconstruction of our country and in achieving internal unity. (Yoshida 1995)

In his succeeding policy speech to the Diet he maintained the same line, bequeathing to posterity the slogan 'General Penitence by the Hundred Million.' This last expression was a customary term for the Japanese nation but was arrived at by counting the colonial subjects in Korea and Taiwan who were of course even less responsible for the war than the mass of ethnic Japanese who lacked any part in decision-making. In contrast to his criticism of the nation, Higashikuni described the termination of the war as due to the Emperor's gracious benevolence. He went on, however, to detail more concrete military reasons for the defeat itself in terms of the vastly discrepant war potentials of Japan and the United States. He thus separated the question of defeat itself, explained in material terms, from that of war responsibility, to be met with collective penitence.

This line provoked an intense double backlash among the public. To begin with, it was now possible to express long-held but smothered resentments of the inequality of sacrifice experienced during the war, when the mass of the people had suffered acute hardship and loss, while senior military and civil officials maintained comfortable and even luxurious lifestyles. So Higashikuni's bracketing of privileged and unprivileged as equally owing penitence was a bitter pill. Regarding the reasons for defeat, too, his revelation of Japan's material inferiority starkly demonstrated the recklessness of the war and the irresponsibility of the leadership who had gambled the country's fate on it.

Reports on public reactions brought statements like 'we now realize the deceitful policy of the leadership who knew the realities of national strength,' 'the leaders who deceived the nation right to the end deserve ten thousand deaths,' and 'before the nation repents, those who had been in charge must themselves take responsibility.' Such reactions happened to coincide with current instructions being issued to the occupation authorities on initial postsurrender policy, which emphasized that the public be made aware of the role of the armed forces leadership and their collaborators to prepare for national re-education and acceptance of the planned war trials of representative figures among that leadership.

Prince Higashikuni resigned after less than two months following the repercussions of a report in the U.S. forces' newspaper *Stars and Stripes* by a British correspondent, relating an interview with the Home Minister. The latter had stated: 'All those who advocate a reform of the political system, especially the abolition of the Emperor system, are Communists and will be arrested under the Peace Preservation Law.' This law had been the main legal basis for ideological suppression and provided for a maximum penalty of death for any who advocated a change in the form of government or opposed the rights of private property. It originally had been aimed at Marxists, though gradually extended to cover any form of dissidence and was administered by a branch of the civil police called the Special Higher Police or the 'thought police,' for their function of prosecuting 'ideological crimes' or 'dangerous thoughts.' In practice, the establishment was usually reluctant to impose the death penalty, particularly as the Special Higher Police achieved considerable success with brainwashing techniques. Dissidents who did not succumb to this treatment were sentenced to life imprisonment and most prisoners of this kind still being held at the end of the war had been underground Communists.

This press report drew the attention of GHQ to the persistence of repressive ideology in the government, which was then ordered to release all political prisoners, abolish the Special Higher Police, dismiss the Home Minister and all officials engaged in repression, and repeal all laws restricting civic freedom. At this Higashikuni realized that the occupation intended to introduce fundamental reforms, even if the Emperor were retained, and resigned rather than preside over such a process.

He was succeeded by Shidehara Kijuro, a member of the House of Peers who obtained the support of the largest group of Lower House members. He was also a logical choice at this juncture since, in the period of liberal ascendancy and party government ended by the Manchurian Incident and right wing terrorism in the early 1930s, he had long served as Foreign Minister and was identified with the conciliatory policies known as 'Shidehara diplomacy.' The parties, though in decline, had continued to dominate Lower House elections until their dissolution in 1940 and now promptly revived. The two main groups reverted to the original names of their forebears in the later 19th century, Progressives and Liberals.

Shidehara now headed a Progressive Party Cabinet and launched a project to set the record straight by setting up a Committee of Inquiry into the War. British and Soviet representatives in the Allied Council, however, objected to its approach, and it was abolished in less than a year. Meanwhile, the Progressive Party, which naturally attracted many opportunists, was badly affected by the first phase of the purge of wartime officeholders in politics and the economy, and, following the first postwar election, Shidehara was replaced by Yoshida Shigeru of the Liberal Party. He was also a career diplomat with a record of opposition to military domination, though socially highly conserva-

6

tive and monarchist. After some vicissitudes, he was to dominate politics in the later phase of the occupation—the 'reverse course.'

During this time, the occupation program of reeducation combined with censorship was taking hold and was to have enduring effects on Japanese perceptions of the war, far beyond the occupation itself. Some early steps were the abolition of the state Shinto cult and the Emperor's 'denial of his divinity' in his New Year message. This was framed under Shidehara's guidance along the lines that 'the ties between us and you as members of the nation have been bound together throughout by mutual trust, respect, and affection and have not arisen through mere myths and legends.' A *Time* correspondent, sampling reactions in street interviews, was baffled to be repeatedly told 'we always knew he wasn't a god.' Actually the Shinto conception of divinity had always been pantheistic, without the Western conception of a definitive gulf between the divine and the human, and it has been common usage to describe outstanding figures as 'god of strategy' or 'god of elections' and so forth, so this exercise was not quite as momentous as conceived in the West. But it was a step to a more democratic conception of the Emperor, suited to the reforms being planned.

Shidehara seems to have had some part, not entirely clear, in framing Article 9 of the new Constitution renouncing war. Although most of this Constitution was drafted by GHQ, there was some Japanese input, and the form presented to the Diet was officially represented as the result of Japanese initiative, so as to avoid criticism of the soundness of a Constitution imposed from outside.

Another step in reeducation was the banning of the term 'Greater East Asia War' because of its ideological implications as to the nature of the war as aimed at the liberation of East Asia from Western colonialism. It was replaced by 'Pacific War,' which was popularized by a U.S.-centered version of the war's history serialized in all newspapers and over Japan's national broadcasting system, designed to 'inform the Japanese nation of the facts of the war and the crimes of the leadership who led Japan to defeat.' It treated the war as beginning in Manchuria in 1931 and excluded any consideration of Japan's colonialism in Taiwan and Korea (since these were acquired in a period of alliance with Britain and U.S. acquiescence). China was treated as a victim of Japanese aggression, but little significance was attached to its war of resistance (in which the Chinese Communists played an important role) even though it involved the largest number of troops in any theater of war. Resistance movements in Southeast Asia were ignored except for the Philippine guerrillas, who were linked to the U.S. effort (though later condemned as Communist). The Emperor, the Court, the Zaibatsu combines, which had done much to mobilize the war economy, and the media were portrayed as 'moderates' overridden by the militarists, mainly in the armed forces, so as to narrow war responsibility to them, though this was by no means wholly accurate. The people's deception by militarists was emphasized with a view to

7

sparing the nation as a whole from a sense of direct blame or rancor which could impede future cooperation with the Western camp in the mounting confrontation with the Communist bloc.

The wholly U.S. centered image of the war which so downplayed the Asian dimension also had the long-term effect of reinforcing the habitual Japanese attitude of contempt for other Asians, which dated from the last century and stemmed from their failure to resist Western colonialism or to modernize their societies as effectively as Japan had been able to do. The classic statement of this outlook, which perpetually recurs in postwar debates on the nature of the war, relations with Asia, and relevant educational issues, is an article written in 1885 by the prominent theorist of modernization Fukuzawa Yukichi, founder of Keio University and co-founder of the original Progressive Party. It is entitled 'Abandoning Asia and Joining Europe' and presents the following argument:

> Although our country is situated at the eastern edge of Asia, the spirit of our people has already abandoned Asia's hidebound ways and embraced Western civilization. We have here two unfortunate neighbor countries—China and Korea. Although their people in former times shared with Japan a similar nurturing in Asian-type doctrines and customs, now, either because of some difference in race or because of some difference in mode within that inherited education ... these do not comprehend the path of national reform.... In framing present policies, we have no leisure to await their awakening and together to revive Asia.... We cannot treat them with special consideration just because they are our neighbors, we must treat them just as Westerners do.

There is still some debate about the precise intent and significance of this article. The immediate occasion for writing it was Fukuzawa's disillusionment over the failure the previous year of an attempted coup by a progressive faction in Korea, which included some former Korean students of his academy. He had entertained hopes that such a movement, along the lines of the Meiji Restoration of 1868 which had overthrown feudalism in Japan, might achieve a similar reform in Korea, which could then form a common front with Japan against Western pressures, then very much in evidence. But the coup was crushed by the reactionary party with Chinese help and Fukuzawa despaired of any common action with Asians. The alternative was for Japan to join the Imperialist Club in the contest for colonial spoils—which became a standard policy in the Japanese establishment.

Even those elements, both liberal and right wing, who retained some genuine hopes for Asian revival leaned to the views that Asia could only be liberated under Japanese hegemony, with Asians as acquiescent clients. This was ultimately the line adopted by the leadership in the Second World War in its declared aim of 'Greater East Asian Co-prosperity.'

The persistence of such an outlook after the war is vividly illustrated by a U.S. survey of attitudes among Japanese residents remaining in Beijing in late 1945. Like the Western colonialists who had always held that the subject peoples were incapable of ruling themselves, 69 percent of respondents did not believe that the Chinese could operate the industries established by Japan in Manchuria; 77 percent believed that the Koreans would not be able to rule themselves for at least 20 years; 50 percent did not believe that China could be described as a real state and 86 percent believed that the Japanese were superior to other Far Eastern nations, though only 41 percent believed that the Japanese were superior to all other races (defeat having somewhat lowered their self-image in relation to the West). (Yoshida 1995)

Such attitudes continued to prevail throughout the Cold War period, as Japan was so closely identified with the Western camp that, except among left wing elements, little need was felt for any independent approach to Asian countries or any serious reflection on Japan's wartime treatment of them. It was only long afterwards, with the decline of the Cold War, that such issues came to life, with some serious consideration of the significance of the war for Asian countries.

During the early years of the occupation, with such unpredictable convulsions in Asia as the Communist victory in China, wars of liberation in former Western colonies, and other complexities, occupation censorship also presented a big deterrent to speculation on such issues. It was significant that, while other areas of occupation policy were implemented indirectly through the Japanese government, direct control was exercised over the media. Prior censorship of the big five Tokyo newspapers began in October and then extended to 60 nationwide. Figures of staff employed in censorship in 1948 included 370 American and 5,700 Japanese.

Newsprint rationing was a potent means of control and procedures used in censoring specific passages caused greater hardship than in wartime Japanese censorship. Whereas the latter had merely deleted offending sections, leaving gaps in the published text, occupation censorship demanded a complete recasting to remove any visible trace, so that editors were compelled to exercise extreme caution to avoid this possibility. As they had during the war, newspapers and press agencies maintained internal precensorship sections which, among other things, collected examples of previously censored items to anticipate similar future action by the authorities.

The guidelines and press code issued were not entirely clear or comprehensive. The initial guidelines aimed mainly at eliminating 'militaristic, feudalistic, or ultranationalist material' but few problems were encountered in this area. Policies here were clear enough, and in any case the changes in management mentioned earlier tended to favor new staff who had little attachment to wartime ideology. Concern therefore came to focus on material that could be construed as critical of occupation or allied policy or highlighted social problems in ways that might favor radicalism or cause unrest. The new management of the *Asahi* moved quickly to resume its traditional reformist role in an editorial declaring its identification with 'the nation at work in factories, workplaces, and farming villages who are truly those to rebuild the newborn Japan' as against 'militarist remnants, aloof intelligentsia, mighty bureaucrats, and unrepentant Zaibatsu.' In a still more dramatic shift, the *Yomiuri* management was taken over by representatives of its trade union when its president was arrested as a war criminal suspect (one of a number of media figures arrested or purged), but its line became so critical of developments under the occupation that GHQ ordered its new management dismissed in mid-1946.

This occurred in a context where an unexpectedly radical labor movement was emerging. The new Constitution had established the rights of organized labor as a 'countervailing force' against future possible reactionary trends, but the American authorities were taken aback by its militancy after its long suppression. It was closely linked with the emerging left wing parties—an only modestly successful Communist Party and a much larger social democratic grouping with a fairly long history as a legal party movement predating the war. This was of course alien to American tradition which has never included parties of this kind, unlike other developed countries. The situation was partly blamed on elements in GHQ staff described as New Dealers, subscribers to the liberal (in U.S. terms) measures introduced by President Roosevelt to overcome the Great Depression. A large-scale replacement of such staff was therefore carried out in May 1946, including the press section head himself, and from this time material viewed as favoring Communism was also made subject to censorship. Antilabor censorship was particularly intensified in the lead-up to the general strike planned for February 1947, which was banned by occupation order. Such concerns of course deepened during the Korean War which began in mid-1950.

Although censorship ended with the occupation, when the new freedoms embodied in the Constitution took full effect, critics of the Japanese press claim that it has never outgrown the cautious habits instilled by both wartime and occupation censorship. Evidence of this is seen in the system of press clubs attached to the various ministries as channels for handouts favoring bureaucratic perspectives. Even after the Peace Treaty, the continuing Security Treaty with the United States also served as an inhibiting factor on any criticism of the official image of the war, so that until related issues reignited in the 1980s the press generally avoided discussion or analysis of Japan's war record, contributing to the public's real or perceived amnesia on the subject.

The centerpiece of this official image of course consisted of the Tokyo Trials of class A war criminals, meaning those accused of 'crimes against peace' in the sense of 'conspiracy to wage aggressive war,' as distinct from classes B and C, tried for ordering or carrying out specific atrocities. Press coverage of all these cases, which extended over about three years, formed the main content of public reeducation on the war. The trials were part of the overall Allied program of defining the exclusive war guilt of the Axis powers. The legal basis was a charter, originally designed for the German case, drawn up at a conference of the Big Four Western allies on the conclusion of the war in Europe. It was necessarily retroactive, since up to that time, in international law, war was regarded as an unqualified sovereign right of the state, and individuals were not treated as personally liable for 'acts of state.' The only approach to a qualification of this right had been the Kellogg-Briand Peace Pact of 1928, whose signatories, including Japan, had agreed to settle problems by peaceful means without resorting to war, but it lacked specifics and the charter was felt to be necessary as a basis for trials at the political level. The B and C class trials were more securely based on the Hague and Geneva conventions governing the conduct of war.

Within the European Axis, although Italy had been the pioneer in fascistic dictatorship and external aggression in Ethiopia, Spain, and Albania, it was not subject to war trials. This was partly because the dictator Mussolini himself had been summarily executed by Communist partisans, along with various other deaths among the leadership; partly because the palace-centered regime which had taken over in the south had declared war on Germany and was then more or less counted among the allies. The German case in contrast was quite clear-cut in view of unchallenged Nazi control throughout and the scale of such enormities as the holocaust carried out against the Jews. The Japanese case had distinctive features again.

In the first place, there was greater difficulty in defining the range of possible guilty parties. As one British observer put it:

> The difficulties of drafting and agreeing on the defendants have been much greater than over the Nuremberg indictment, in that Japan never had any consistent party like the Nazis, and out of a plethora of possible defendants responsible since 1931, only a few can be picked from a very competitive bunch. (Williams et al. 1989)

An index of the intense factional conflicts, punctuated by high-level assassinations, which occupied the decade leading up to Pearl Harbor, is provided by the frequency of cabinet changes. In the five years from the attempted coup by army dissidents in 1936, which under emergency provisions shifted power decisively to the military, there were eight changes of cabinet with varying line-ups of army, navy, and bureaucratic cliques. The Tojo cabinet represented the last critical phase in a crescendo of internal struggle and international escalation—'a process, full of vicissitudes, emerging from the historical potential of diverse confrontations, conflicts and compromises within ruling circles,' as one Japanese commentator has put it. (Nikkan 1993)

In the second place, and ironically, the only constant figure through these vicissitudes, was the Emperor himself, whom the U.S. authorities had decided to exclude from consideration for the reasons mentioned, despite disagreement among some of the allies. Unlike the situation at Nuremberg where the Big

11

Four exercised joint control, the United States had sole control of trial procedures, including the appointment of all judges and the chief prosecutor. The Cold War had also progressed further than at Nuremberg and exerted a growing influence over the much more protracted Tokyo trials. One example was that from May 1947, the defense was allowed more scope for the admission of evidence unfavorable to the Soviet Union than applied to other countries.

Although the Japanese government in the Peace Treaty with the Western allies was obliged to accept the verdict of the trials and was never much disposed to reopen it as an issue, both the right and left wings have resented the procedure for opposite reasons. The right condemns it as victor's justice, where one side was both prosecutor and judge. In this view, the war was Japan's legitimate attempt to break out of encirclement by Western imperialism, finally provoked by the oil embargo in mid-1941. The left, on the other hand, condemns the trials as inadequate, representing them as a bargain struck between the United States and Japanese establishment to spare the Emperor, along with the whole Imperial House and most nonmilitary ruling circles, including the Zaibatsu, for purely political ends.

Although a considerable section of even conservative opinion favored the Emperor's abdication in the interests of a new start, GHQ refused to countenance it. It has been a universal custom in Japanese public life that the head of an organization resigns as atonement or apology for any sort of failure, even if solely due to subordinates, and some of the military are said to have expected this of their 'commander-in-chief.' One conservative spokesman held that his failure to accept moral (if not legal) responsibility for the war would weaken the Imperial House in the future. A *Yomiuri* survey in 1948 found that, at that late stage in the trials, 18 percent of the public favored abdication and 4 percent (no doubt Communist) the abolition of the monarchy itself. Another survey among professional and public figures found that 51 percent in politics, law, or public office favored abdication, together with 49 percent of those associated with education or religion, though only 15 percent of those in the financial field did. But at the same period, General MacArthur himself was personally involved with dissuading the Emperor from any thought of abdication, which he seemed to be contemplating.

Regarding actual trial procedure, one criticism is that only three of the 11 judges were Asian (from China, India, and the Philippines), which also tended to minimize Asia's importance in the Japanese image of the war. The question of Japan's earlier colonization of Taiwan and Korea was never raised for reasons suggested earlier, as this had been part of the mutually recognized colonial order dominated by the Western powers. This was a particularly sensitive issue at the time, when wars of liberation were being fought. Another criticism was of the sweeping rulings of inadmissibility of much of the evidence sought to be tendered by the defense, eight volumes of which, preserved in the Justice Ministry, were later published by a right wing academic. Still another criticism concerned discontinuities of attendance by many of the judges, a simple majority of the 11 constituted the quorum for a session.

Oral testimony played a large part as vast amounts of documentation been destroyed by the Foreign Ministry and other government agencies im mediately after the surrender. Although considerable information about the origins and conduct of the war was presented, this could hardly be entirely balanced and comprehensive, even in terms of the time available, and much remained to be explored and debated by later research. The defense of course was at a great disadvantage even from the strictly procedural standpoint, as the charge, virtually in effect an assumption, of a general conspiracy was so diffuse as to be hardly possible to rebut.

The verdicts, however, were not unanimous as six different opinions were returned among the 11 judges. Two found the defendants not guilty—Justice Pal of India on the grounds that the war was one of resistance to Western domination of Asia, which had involved his own country, also that retroactive law was invalid, and Bernard of France, on the grounds of defective trial procedures, as well as the Emperor's arbitrary exclusion. The trials were, however, regarded by GHQ as serving their purpose, both educational and punitive. Of the total class A suspects, 28 had been initially indicted while another 17 had been held for future trials which were never held. Of those tried, seven were executed, including of course Tojo, while 16 others were sentenced to life imprisonment, though these were released on the agreement of the Western allies after the Peace Treaty. Of the other six executed, all but one were former army officers. One was also linked with the 'Rape of Nanking,' the customary term for the slaughter and pillage that had accompanied the fall of Nanking, the Nationalist Chinese capital in late 1937. The details and significance of this event have remained a key theme in later debates about the war. Another class A suspect was linked with the Burma-Thailand railway, an episode in the war made notorious for its human rights violations and brutality towards prisoners of war.

The only civilian executed, despite a dissenting finding of not guilty by Justice Roeling of the Netherlands, was Hirota Koki, a career diplomat who had headed the cabinet that followed the 1936 attempted military coup. His use of an inner cabinet of five key ministers to cope with the current emergency was regarded as having a 'conspiratorial' character. His government also concluded the Anti-Comintern Pact with Germany, foreshadowing the later Axis alliance, though initially directed towards combating the communist Third International based on Moscow. This was, at the time, the establishment's most acute concern, especially in view of the growing strength of the Chinese communists.

At this juncture, however, further trials for cases still outstanding in all three classes were abandoned as part of policies introduced under the U.S. National Security Report 13/2 of October 1948, which also signaled the depurge of wartime office-holders, the abandonment of earlier plans for

13

Zaibatsu dissolution and in general making explicit the 'reverse course' of occupation policies. A radically new emphasis was placed on Japan's economic recovery and ultimate rearmament even at the cost of reform in order to relieve the financial burden of occupation and the possible defense of Japan against subversion or attack.

Among the 17 class A suspects released was Kishi Nobusuke, who had been a close associate of Tojo since their earlier days in Manchukuo, the client state that served as a laboratory for the political and economic totalitarianism that was later applied in Japan. He was Minister for Commerce and Industry in the Pearl Harbor cabinet and thus responsible for the wartime mobilization of the economy. His role had certainly been far more crucial than Hirota's, yet he was not only released but within less than ten years had become prime minister—the most spectacular manifestation of the 'reverse course.'

Another difference from Germany was the absence of any Japanese attempt to supplement the Allied run trials by others on Japanese initiative on the grounds of damage suffered by Japan itself and attributed to the wartime leadership. The assistant chief council for the defense, Kiyose Ichiro, recognized this aspect in his opening address at the trial:

> If internal war crimes trials were to be undertaken in this country, calling to account the responsibility of Tojo, Matsuoka [former pro-Axis foreign minister] and the rest for bringing Japan to this pass, I would not by any means argue their innocence. If these present trials were also concerned with their responsibility to this country, we defense council ourselves would take a different attitude from what we do today. My position, however, is that, since these trials are of an international character, I intend to devote what efforts I am capable of to reveal to the world the position that our country occupied in the past.... (Yoshida 1995)

The U.S. authorities, however, would not have favored any such disturbance to Cold War solidarity as further trials and a survey in 1955 found that only 31 percent of respondents favored any such action—mainly the same groups as those who had favored the Emperor's abdication.

One last omission from war crimes trials which came as a great shock when revealed many years later was the exemption from prosecution of Unit 731 which, with its main base in Manchuria and other stations in Japan, China, and Southeast Asia, had for many years conducted the world's most highly coordinated research program on biological and chemical warfare, involving experiments, including vivisection, on thousands of captives. It has been described by a later Japanese commentator as 'the greatest shame even among Japan's war crimes.' Comparable German activities, which seem to have been less coordinated, had been immediately exposed in Europe, but when Unit 731 and its gruesome record became known to occupation intelligence, they were kept secret and the immunity from prosecution of its staff ensured by General

MacArthur directly, in exchange for their data and further assistance to American projects in these fields. As U.S. researchers commented, 'such information could not be obtained in our laboratories because of scruples attached to human experimentation.' (Williams et al. 1989) The impact of this unit's exposure and issues involving it belong to a later chapter.

The 'reverse course' was firmly set following the Communist victory in China in 1949. Some American commentators on this dramatic development expressed regret, from the Cold War perspective, that shortsighted U.S. policies in the past had contributed to the Communist success. It was argued that if, in the 1930s the United States had better appreciated Japan's difficulties in the crisis posed by the Depression and extreme protectionism in the world economy, it might have been possible to mediate between Japan and Nationalist China rather than unconditionally backing the latter. This in turn could have led to a three-fold combined front capable of defeating Communism in China. It would of course, if possible, have also averted the Pacific War itself—an implication favoring right wing arguments that the United States shared some blame for the war.

Up to the Communist victory, the United States had hoped that the Chinese Nationalist regime could contain the spread of Communism in Asia, and when this prospect collapsed Japan became not only a client needing to help defend itself but the West's sole reliable 'bulwark against Communism' in Asia. By now, after a brief interval of Socialist and Democratic (formally Progressive) cabinets, Yoshida and the Liberal Party were securely in control of the Diet and, together with the reviving establishment, fully in accord with the 'bulwark' doctrine. Yoshida did subsequently resist U.S. pressures for extensive rearmament out of genuine fear of revived militarism, which he had always opposed. But on the home front he was fully committed to the suppression of left wing dissidence and under the Organization Control Ordinance presided over the 'Red Purge,' under which thousands of leftists and labor militants were dismissed from both public and private employment. The Korean minority's schools, to some extent linked with left wing influence, were suppressed. Later, purge by occupation order, originally introduced to counter ultranationalism, was applied in reverse to expel 35 elected Communist members from the Diet, some of whom found their way to China.

Although Britain and some other Western countries, in accordance with normal international practice, extended *de facto* recognition to the Chinese Communist regime once it was clearly in control, the United States never recognized the distinction between *de facto* and *de jure* recognition, so in effect it did not recognize the new regime's existence. This meant that China could no longer be party to an overall peace treaty with Japan. Although remnants of the Nationalist regime were holding out in Taiwan, their viability was in some doubt, particularly in view of their very bad relations with the local inhabitants, while this regime could also hardly fit into a treaty framework with other allies who no longer recognized it as the government of China.

The most intense debate since the war erupted within Japan over the admissibility or desirability of a partial peace treaty excluding China and potentially other former allies sympathetic to China, especially as such a peace would tie Japan exclusively to the Western camp and allow the retention of U.S. bases in Japan. At the beginning of 1950, a Peace Question Symposium, which included prominent intellectuals such as Nambara Shigeru, President of Tokyo University, issued a statement attacking proposals for a separate peace. Expressing 'self-criticism for losing the opportunity to decide our own destiny for ourselves at the outbreak of war' and 'with the intent of atoning for past war responsibility,' the statement declared:

> For a peace treaty to hold its true significance, it must be complete, both in form and substance. If not, though it might purport to be a peace treaty, it will in fact on the contrary increase the risk of war anew.... It must be viewed as a proper demand that Japan, having accepted the Potsdam Declaration, seek the recovery of peaceful relations with all the allies. (Rekishi Kyoikusha Kyogikai 1995)

Professor Nambara took the same stand in attending an educational conference in the United States and later elaborated his group's arguments at a graduation ceremony for the young elite who would soon be rising to positions of influence, always dominated by his university's graduates. He noted that the recently concluded Sino-Soviet Treaty of Alliance had the stated aim of 'preventing a revival of Japanese imperialism and any new aggression by Japan or any country in league with Japan.' But he also noted statements by both U.S. and Soviet spokesmen expressing hopes for the coexistence of both blocs and argued that Japan could occupy a special position in facilitating such coexistence, both by its strategic location and by virtue of its constitutional renunciation of war. This, if Japan persisted in neutrality, could give it a moral weight disproportionate to its current total lack of military capability. He therefore eloquently opposed a separate peace as 'bondage' to one camp, with its implication of hypothetical enemies.

> The absence of a great ideal means the death of a race. May not the Japanese nation, awakening from its one-time nightmare of the Greater East Asia Coprosperity Sphere, now live for the great and radiant ideal of permanent world peace, directed by reason and truth? (*Bungei Shunju* 1995).

The symposium's stand was naturally backed by the left wing parties, organized labor, and religious bodies. The Democratic Party for its part condemned Yoshida's secret negotiations, which concealed the true situation from the people, and joined the Socialists in a statement calling for permanent neutrality. Yoshida counterattacked at a general meeting of Liberal Diet members,

16

stating that neutrality could only be obtained by concluding appropriate treaties with other countries and that it was self-evident whether this was possible at present. He condemned Professor Nambara's statement in the United States as 'the empty rhetoric of an academic who twists learning to fawn on current fads.' Yoshida claimed to aim at 'peace by practical stages' and gave economic recovery an overriding priority. In practical terms, this was only possible in close association with the Western economies, which developed into Japan's dominant postwar policy known as the 'Yoshida Doctrine,' meaning sole concern with economic success and strictly defensive military capability with U.S. backup.

Any possibility of an overall peace that might have existed was ruled out by the Korean war which began in mid-year, with the United States and China as the key combatants. After that, despite a continuing pacifist and neutralist movement which has persisted ever since with occasional effectiveness, developments led inevitably to the partial peace treaty concluded at San Francisco in 1951, with its corollary of the Japan-U.S. Security Treaty.

Neither Chinese regime was invited to the peace conference. Newly independent India and Burma, with Yugoslavia, refused attendance on the grounds that the Security Treaty represented a continuation of Western imperialist interference in Asia. The Soviet Union, Poland, and Czechoslovakia attended but refused to sign for the same reason. The treaty therefore lost any real character of liquidation of war responsibility but rather became an induction into the Western camp. Japan was required to accept the verdict of the Tokyo trials but with the implication that this settled the question of war responsibility.

Most significantly, the Western allies relinquished all claims to reparations in the interests of Japan maintaining viability in its 'bulwark' role. The treaty, while noting that Japan ought to pay reparations for the 'loss and suffering' inflicted through the war, went on to recognize that 'Japan's resources are at present inadequate to make full reparation for the loss and suffering referred to and at the same time fulfill its other obligations.' It was provided that other countries could enter into bilateral negotiations for reparations with Japan but that these should not exceed Japan's capacity to pay. It might be noted that, in the immediate aftermath of war, the United States had planned to reduce Japan to an 'Asian level standard of living,' which seems to assume that Asians would always be impoverished colonial subjects, but this was obviously incompatible with Japan's new (or rather restored) role of ally of the West and any such idea was strictly buried.

Any reparations agreed to would not be by monetary payment but in products or services financed internally in Japan. Agreements in the form of reparations were later reached with Burma, the Philippines, Indonesia, and South Vietnam. Other similar arrangements with Asian countries were framed in terms of economic cooperation or aid, as in the separate peace treaties concluded with the Chinese Nationalists and India, the normalization treaty with South Korea, and later agreements with other countries.

17

In Prime Minister Yoshida's address to the peace conference, he described the treaty as 'not a treaty of revenge but a document of reconciliation and trust, which the Japanese plenipotentiaries are gratified to accept.' He expressed regret at the absence of India and Burma and that China had been 'unable to attend,' but he went on to add in justification of the Security Treaty:

> Sinister forces associated with communist oppression and despotism are spreading unrest and disorder in the Far East and engaging in overt aggression everywhere. These forces are pressing close on Japan. But the Japanese nation has no armaments and against this collective onslaught has no other recourse than to seek collective protection from the other free nations. (*Bungei Shunju* 1995)

He closed with something of an apology for the war:

> We have heard the plenipotentiaries of various countries recollect the terrible suffering and enormous material destruction undergone by humanity during the Pacific War and we recollect with feelings of sorrow the role played by the old Japan in those great disasters for mankind.

His appreciation of the 'generous peace' was echoed immediately afterwards by the chairman of a general meeting of the Federation of Economic Organizations (Keidanren) in the words: 'considering the present international situation, feelings towards Japan and the crimes that Japan has committed, we may describe this as the most generous peace that could possibly be hoped for.' (Yoshida 1995)

A more radical commentator puts the same general idea differently. He contrasts the case of Germany, which was thoroughly 'hit back' on its own territory by the nations whom Germany had invaded, with Japan, which was spared this fate by being protected as a bulwark against Communism by the United States, which on its own home territory (presumably excluding Hawaii as then a colony) was only hit by toy-like balloon bombs. 'It is true that Japan suffered air raids and atomic bombs, but this was not a matter of being "hit back" by the Asian countries which it had "hit," but by America, which was no more than the same sort of aggressor against Asia.' (Honda 1991)

In any case, the whole combination of circumstances surrounding the war's end, the occupation, and its conclusion dominated the common Japanese perception of the Asia-Pacific War during most of the succeeding Cold War and only began to be widely questioned when the latter had virtually ended.

2 Through the high growth period (1952-1972)

After the Peace Treaty took effect in 1952, 'reverse course' policies were strengthened still further. Internally, the Organizations Control Ordinance was replaced by a more comprehensive Subversive Activities Prevention Law, followed by a partial recentralization of the police force, which occupation reforms had placed under local government control as the alternative to the earlier harsh police regime. Externally, policies for Japan's rearmament were discussed at the Ikeda-Robertson talks in Washington in 1953. Here the Japanese representatives countered U.S. demands for extensive rearmament by detailing four constraints presented by the internal situation in Japan.

The first was legal, under Article 9 of the U.S.-imposed constitution, which ruled out armament of any kind. Amendment was subject to a difficult process which could not be realized in the near future, even if the leadership accepted it as necessary. Economic constraints were also a factor, although Japan's ultimate recovery had been given its start by the Korean War. Political and social constraints arose from public attitudes molded by the occupation's antimilitaristic educational policies, though of course also reinforced by painful memories of what militarism had brought to Japan. The educational factor was especially strong among the generation now coming of age who had been mainly educated under the occupation.

The Japanese representatives, however, concluded a secret agreement to introduce a public reeducation program (or re-reeducation) reversing that of the occupation in order to cultivate patriotism and defense-mindedness. The agreement was exposed by the *Asahi,* now fully restored to its traditional role of left-liberal criticism of establishment policies. (Rekishi Kyoikusha 1995) Such a program was, however, pursued by the authorities who also had their own additional reasons for attempting to revive a nationalistic spirit. The prevailing sense in Japan of being completely subordinated to U.S. policies was felt as harmful to national morale by all segments of society in various ways, whether left wing, right wing, or pragmatic mainstream.

19

In the following year, legislation established Self-Defense Forces with strictly defensive capabilities but more clearly military in character than the National Police Reserve introduced during the Korean War. In the same year, a law was passed to enforce political neutrality in compulsory education (to year nine). Though framed in terms of neutrality, this measure was in practical effect aimed against left wing or pacifistic bias in education, a trend already marked in the teaching profession.

The very complex issues involving education will be studied later. Meanwhile, a more general reorientation of public attitudes was being attempted by the authorities, largely centered as in the past on the Imperial House. The task was simplified by the fusion of the Liberal and Democratic Parties as the LDP in 1955, so inaugurating this party's long hold on power, known as the '1955 system,' lasting until 1993.

Without constitutional amendment, the Emperor's limited role as 'symbol of the state and of the unity of the people' could not be altered but much could be done within this framework. The media's role was, of course, crucial. The authorities no longer had any power to impose any particular line on the latter which, however, as usual tended to reflect the mood of the establishment and, as earlier suggested, had perhaps been tamed by the long experience of wartime and occupation censorship. So, while still preserving the newer image of the Emperor in a democratic setting, something of the old mystique was revived. The media continued to refer to him in high honorifics, which can be very elaborate in Japanese, though not to the extreme suggesting divinity that had once prevailed. A negative motive was also provided by the continuing threat of ultranationalist groups who have repeatedly resorted to 'righteous' violence against anyone accused of disrespect to the Emperor or their conception of Japan's honor. Such groups have also often had covert links to the LDP and been used for purposes with which the party would not wish to be publicly involved though exposed on a number of occasions and ultimately contributing to the party's loss of power much later.

In any case, media coverage had the effect of distancing the Emperor from political controversy and possible criticism, especially as all news concerning the Imperial family was channeled through the Imperial Household Agency which naturally left no opening for criticism. As the war period became more remote and the level of prosperity reached unprecedented heights, nostalgia for traditional ideals also played its part. As the very deep-rooted Japanese propensity for hierarchy in all contexts reemerged after postwar fluidity, the Emperor could regain his role as the apex of all hierarchies. He could also serve as the focus for the preservation of traditional culture, which indeed had been the court's only function during the long centuries of feudal domination by the shoguns.

Although the State Shinto cult had been abolished, the Emperor continued to observe or authorize traditional rituals at shrines historically associated with the Imperial House, the Shinto ritualists being treated as court employees rather than public servants. He also made private visits to the Yasukuni Shrine to the war dead and regularly sent imperial messages to its twice yearly festivals. In his periodic tours of the countryside, originally promoted by the occupation authorities to cultivate a democratic image, he was now greeted by local Defense Force units and senior officers were later granted the right of audience. A reported discussion with the Director of the Defense Agency provided a rare occasion for criticism of the Emperor as improperly venturing into the political realm. But most of his activities were reported in such a way as to make the public feel involved as part of the national identity so symbolized. The use of the national flag and the highly monarchist national anthem were encouraged, especially in schools, though this long remained voluntary and was resisted by the Teacher's Union.

After Yoshida lost power in 1954, his three successors were all formerly purged prewar politicians, the last being Kishi who, as mentioned, had figured in the Tojo cabinet and been listed as a class A war criminal before the trials were cut short. When he became Prime Minister in 1957, his government attempted to go beyond purely symbolic measures with institutional initiatives marking the ultimate limit of reactionary trends under the 'reverse course,' until growing resistance over a wide spectrum of society, including media and elements of his own highly factionalized party, halted the process. A bill for a much strengthened police system and attempts to revise the Constitution both failed.

The climax was reached in 1960 surrounding the scheduled renewal of the Security Treaty with the United States. To overcome intense opposition, ostensibly to treaty renewal but more essentially to Kishi's policies generally, he arranged for President Eisenhower to visit Japan and be received at the airport by the Emperor on the eve of the Diet session called to ratify the renewal. This plan, however, was canceled because of the tumultuous antitreaty demonstrations in Tokyo, led by students. Six days before the President's intended arrival, his press secretary was surrounded by protesters and Kishi had to admit that he could not guarantee the President's safety, or even the Emperor's. This spectacle of an American President's planned visit of support for a leading member of the Pearl Harbor cabinet is surely one of the supreme ironies of modern history! Kishi forced ratification through the Diet by irregular procedures but was then obliged to resign, as well as being subsequently wounded by a right wing fanatic for not being ruthless enough. Some of the right wing had offered to act as storm troopers to clear the way but such a spectacle would have been even more damaging than the cancellation. The leader of the Socialist Party was soon afterwards assassinated at a rally with television coverage by another rightist.

Power then swung back decisively to the 'Yoshida School' of ex-bureaucrat politicians who long remained securely in control, setting aside ideological extremes in favor of concentration on pragmatic 'economism.' It is true that nationalistic sentiment was still cultivated, but the promotion of national prestige was now identified with the conspicuously high rate of economic growth achieved during this period. It was supplemented by some occasions for patriotic sentiment, such as War Dead Commemoration Day on 15 August, introduced in 1963, and the revival of the traditional National Foundation Day, commemorating the accession of the legendary first Emperor.

On the first War Dead Commemoration Day, Prime Minister Ikeda introduced a new note of positive evaluation of the sacrifices of war: 'Since the war, our country has accomplished remarkable cultural and economic development on a peaceful basis, but we must not forget that underlying it were the hopes of many who fell in the firm conviction of the glory of the fatherland.' (Yoshida 1955)

This was an early example of a trend among some of the establishment, as well as the right wing, to credit Japan's wartime efforts (even if in a tortuously oblique sense) for the much improved position enjoyed by postwar Japan—a view so much at variance with the official, totally negative 'Tokyo Trial view of history' as to constitute the beginnings of what one commentator calls the 'double standard.'

Official attempts to rehabilitate a nationalistic spirit were paralleled by some more spontaneous popular developments reflecting a revival of concerns with the war, although on very varied lines. One was a widespread movement for the release of war criminals still serving prison terms, in some cases for life. At the end of 1953, a mass meeting to demand this was held in Tokyo, involving 13,000 representatives of local organizations, who presented petitions carrying 30 million signatures. This movement was reflected in the Diet, which on several occasions up to 1955 passed resolutions for the release of war criminals, opposed only by the Communist Party. These resolutions, however, were not particularly political in aim, as they did not primarily concern A class convicts, whose responsibility for the war was not much questioned, but classes B and C.

One argument used to justify the latters' release was that they were essentially carrying out their duties as determined by their superiors. Another argument emphasized that the trials had been even more arbitrary and selective than the Tokyo Trials. Theirs had been conducted in court martial fashion by local units who had custody of them. As is well known, military law contrasts with civil law in that its primary purpose is not justice for its own sake, with customary safeguards, but the enforcement of control for military ends. So the proceedings tend to be rather summary, perhaps still more so when the accused is not a member of the force. An *Asahi* journalist covering trials by the Dutch in Indonesia criticized the proceedings because:

> They pronounced the death sentence without allowing a defense; the proceedings were conducted in Dutch, prisoners were only allowed to answer yes or no and if they tried to add explanations they were threatened with immediate execution; medicines were withheld from sick

Japanese prisoners; the judge verbally abused defendants and their lawyers. (S. F. Huie, *The Forgotten Ones* Sydney 1992)

The whole issue was, however, settled before long by agreement from the
Western allies to remit outstanding sentences.

On a much larger and more continuing scale in the public arena were recur-
rent booms in literature dealing with the war—some factual, some fictionalized or semifictional, some concentrating on dramatic effect, some nostalgic,
some patriotic, and some antiwar in sentiment. The first boom climaxed following the ratification of the Peace Treaty, after a build-up from the time of
the Korean War. Writings in this period, which included 126 in book form
over 1950-53, were dominated by former staff-class officers. These were
highly professional in treatment, concentrating on set-piece, mechanized aspects of the war rather than on more irregular, guerrilla type operations which
had been prominent in China and the Philippines. They also showed no
awareness of nonprofessional aspects of the war, political, social, or moral.

A prominent example was Tsuji Masanobu, a roving staff planning officer
who had been so ubiquitous on many fronts of the war that he became known
as the 'god of strategy.' He was also directly involved in notorious massacres
of Singapore Chinese, Filipinos, and other cases but had escaped the war trial
proceedings by remaining in China for some time after the war as an advisor
to Chinese nationalists. His accounts of the war completely ignored these latter aspects, as well as his earlier record in the Army General Staff, where he
pressed his superiors to adopt warlike postures at the policy-making level.
This was common in the armed forces and later helped to obscure the real locus of war responsibility, even perhaps to the actors themselves.

In the later 1950s, a contrasting form of reminiscences by more junior officers and noncommissioned officers appeared in magazine form. A prominent
vehicle was the magazine *Maru,* originally a general interest publication
which from 1956 began to specialize in war literature. A special issue of accounts of naval and air war carried the following note:

> Since the war we have tended to be subject to a sense of inferiority
> internationally, but the history of the war we fought against the world's
> greatest powers was, at some stages, not necessarily a story of defeat.
> There was in some cases no lack of signal success that can only lighten
> our hearts. I do not believe that we should ever forget these facts.
> (Yoshida 1995)

Another such periodical, in pamphlet format, was *Current Topics: War
Stories.* After its first few years, it was expanded into a general magazine on
military topics, but a study of the individual accounts of war experience
forming its content up to then indicates that the writers were mainly of junior
rank, with a majority from the navy. Of army accounts, most related to air

war. All tended to emphasize courage and devotion to duty. In the readers' column, however, there was sometimes expressed a dissatisfaction with more ambitious contemporary accounts of the war.

Some examples are:

> In the war literature now so fashionable, most pieces are by higher-ups such as the then commanding officers or unit officers but fewer records born of the misery tasted in the war by common troops in the lower orders. I have never seen one written by air force ground crew [which the writer had been]. Responsibility for the war itself belongs, I believe, to the leadership stratum, but I do not think that those engaged in actual combat had any other idea than that of 'guarding the fatherland.'
>
> There seems to be a boom in the war literature lately, triumphantly issued by members of the high command or staff officers in rear areas, but below these was the sacrifice of myriads of troops engaged in the front line. (Yoshida 1995)

Accounts from common ground troops did emerge a little later but initially were not prominent for various reasons. One was that these had tasted the horrors of war so much more directly that it required more time for them to come to terms with their experiences, even to themselves. Another was that, as emerged later, some came to develop feelings of guilt or regret about their experiences which would have made for less comfortable reading than dashing exploits in the navy or air force. Again, occupation reeducation had so focused public consciousness on the 'Pacific War' aspect that there was little awareness of the Asian dimension of the war, apart from those who had experienced it. There were no accounts of the China front in the accounts published in *Current Topics*.

A systematic attempt to broaden the coverage of the war was made by the quality magazine *Bungei Shunju*. In response to unfavorable reactions to an earlier special issue of war memoirs by high ranking officers, who were accused of 'not reflecting on their responsibility for the defeat,' this magazine tried to balance the picture by calling for accounts from ordinary conscripts, from whom about a thousand manuscripts were collected. The selection published carried an introduction to the effect that it had 'concentrated on memoirs by citizen soldiers who had fought desperate battles in the front line and was dedicated to bereaved families.'

A more scholarly and analytical publication from a Marxist viewpoint was the *History of Showa* (the Emperor's reign title surveyed to date) of 1955 by Toyama Shigeki and others which became a best seller and remained a standard reference. It particularly concentrated on the question of why efforts or elements which might have prevented the war were ineffective. It was written not only to counter the 'self-serving or biased accounts of the war' that had been appearing but, more relevantly to the contemporary scene, to counter the current reactionary political trends that culminated in Kishi's return to power.

Fresh accounts of wartime atrocities, in this case in Manchuria, first prominently emerged in a six volume series in novelized form published from 1956 by Gomikawa Jumpei. He had held a below-officer rank and included vivid accounts of the brutalizing of lower ranks by the higher in the prevalent 'transfer of oppression' or pecking order. In the following year, these themes were extended in more strictly factual terms to the China front in *The Three Lightnings* (Sanko) by Tominaga Shozo, who later helped organize a China Returnees Liaison Council. 'Three Lightnings' was the term applied by the Chinese to the Japanese army's three-fold 'search and destroy' campaign against guerrillas and villages suspected of sheltering them in North China— summed up as 'burn all, kill all, pillage all.' It included accounts, not spoken of since wartime, of the widespread practice of toughening new recruits by having them behead at least one captive by sword. These were received both with shock among readers ignorant of such practices and by accusations of 'shamelessness' from right wing elements. Such revelations as these no doubt contributed to the antiwar movement that helped to topple Kishi.

The most ambitious war studies in this period, which are regarded as approximately mainstream attitudes, were those by Ito Masanori, a former naval war correspondent. These began with *The End of the Combined Fleet,* which was followed by the five volume *The End of the Imperial Army.* Ito consistently recognized that the war could not be justified and that the war in China was the basic cause of the Pacific War. At the same time, he narrows blame to a minority militaristic clique and gives full credit to the sacrificial spirit and patriotism of the mass of the armed forces. There is also a note of nostalgia for the 'glorious' combined fleet. Ito still tends to underrate the full significance of the war in China and describes the bewilderment of the Japanese forces there at the end of the war when they were obliged to surrender to an enemy whom they had consistently defeated in '51 out of 55 battles, with one defeat and three drawn.' In this calculation, of course, he omits the guerrilla war, fought mainly against the Communists, as this was not easily categorized in his conventional, professional approach to military operations.

After Kishi's fall and with the striking success of the 'Yoshida schools' high economic growth policies, a clearer awareness prevailed that the 'postwar adjustment period' was over. Japan's entry into the United Nations in 1956 and the Tokyo Olympic Games in 1964 were the clearest international signs of this. It naturally brought different perspectives to war literature, of which a rather new development was its spread among media catering to juveniles, whether magazines, comics, or other. The content was of course mainly fictionalized, though some factual information on war was included. The main boom in this field lasted through the 1960s.

In the adult field, critics noted a decline in such features of earlier war literature as graphic descriptions of combat and condemnation of aspects of war

25

or policy, with an increasing tendency to idealize the motives and sacrifice of fighting men. This approach, it is suggested, bore an underlying relationship to the efforts Japan was then collectively making to become an 'economic great power' so that the recollection of wartime dedication was regarded as contributing to its renewal or sublimation in a new form.

A major exception at this stage was a four volume series, written by a former war correspondent and published by the *Bungei Shunju,* dealing with the singularly reckless and disastrous invasion of India in the Imphal area in 1944. It was both highly authentic and bitterly critical of the army. Rather comparable was a collection by the *Asahi Weekly* entitled *Father's War Record,* containing 50 pieces selected from a total of 1,716 submitted for a commemoration issue of the 25th anniversary of the end of the war. It contrasted with the earlier *Current Topics* material in that it largely covered the war in China, with none of the earlier publications' dashing exploits by sea or air. There were many expressions of regret for deeds committed and of a wish to apologize to China, though here too the tone is described as less challenging than some earlier material.

Further awareness of the Japanese Army's record in China was stimulated by reflections on its parallels to the then current war in Vietnam. Its 'search and destroy' missions and body counts were reminiscent of the notorious methods of the 'Three Lightnings,' with huge loss of life and burning by napalm of villages suspected of harboring Vietcong guerrillas. The third lightning, 'pillage,' was later referred to by a commentator as having been in any case unnecessary from the U.S. army's point of view as, unlike the poorly supplied Japanese in China, the latter had no need for any resources available in the Vietnamese countryside. One of the memorable war photographs of the time depicted an allied soldier using a cigarette lighter to set fire to a village granary to deny its use to the Vietcong.

The United States attempted to obtain Japanese military participation to join the other auxiliaries from South Korea, the Philippines, Australia, and New Zealand but was again refused on the grounds of Article 9. The Japanese economy, however, profited from logistic support and the U.S. forces under the Security Treaty were entitled to use Japanese bases, mainly in Okinawa which had remained under U.S. military administration. This meant that Japan's involvement was close enough to stimulate a domestic campaign against it, which was actually a continuation of the same coalition of activists who had helped to unseat Kishi. It took organized form from April 1965 as the 'Citizens' League for Peace in Vietnam' (Beheiren) with the slogans 'Peace in Vietnam,' 'Vietnam for the Vietnamese,' and 'No Japanese government collaboration in the war!' It maintained a vigorous and widespread program of activities until 1974, when all foreign combat troops had been withdrawn from Vietnam. It produced a weekly periodical, organized 'teach-ins' of the kind well known elsewhere in the Vietnam War era, aided dissident Vietnamese students, and assisted U.S. army deserters to take refuge in Europe, where the Vietnam War was universally unpopular.

The League placed an antiwar advertisement in the *New York Times* on 16 November 1965, which began by stating that a survey by the *Asahi* in August had found that 94 percent of respondents were seriously concerned about the Vietnam War and 60 percent were afraid of Japan's involvement in it. With reference to Japan's wartime experience in China:

> We have realized, as a result of fifteen years of cruel fighting in China, that this whole question will be decided when it is realized that the people's hearts cannot be won by weapons. This principle is simple but for that very reason is most profound and powerful. It marks the conclusion of all argument on practical policies. Whatever ideals it may be based on, America cannot win the hearts of the Vietnamese people while military action continues. (*Bungei Shunju* 1995)

The *Asahi* survey also found that 75 percent of respondents opposed the saturation bombing of North Vietnam—by far the heaviest in history. A later *Yomiuri* survey in 1968 found that 45 percent of respondents hoped for a compromise solution to the war and 30 percent a conclusion by any means whatever. Of the few clearly taking sides, 6 percent, doubtless Communists and some League members, hoped for a North Vietnam-Vietcong victory and only 3 percent hoped for a U.S. victory. This and other analyses indicate that, while the activist element in the League opposed Japanese military participation as likely to lead to a repetition by Japanese forces of earlier atrocities committed against Chinese, the majority of its sympathizers were afraid rather that involvement in a larger war might lead to a repetition of the suffering experienced by Japanese in the Pacific War. Antiwar feeling tended to stem from the latter concern rather than from the former motive of conscience—an example of prevailing 'victim consciousness' rather than 'aggressor consciousness.'

Noting this implication, an *Asahi* editorial on the 25th anniversary of the end of the war for the first time emphasized the need for Japan to recognize itself in the role of inflictor of harm on Asia rather than, as usual, a sufferer of harm from the United States. Failure to do so was producing a major gap in perception of the war between Japan and the other Asian societies. The right wing viewed this as 'Communist inspired.'

This same period, however, also saw the first conspicuous example of the right wing revisionism that in later years has become more elaborated. Some examples, as in this first case, are distinguished from earlier hangovers from simple wartime patriotism in having wider historical perspectives and a broader range of ideological reference.

This pioneering example was a series of pieces in the quality magazine *Chuo Koron* over 1963 to 1965 under the title *Affirmation of the Greater East*

Asia War by Hayashi Fusao. Around 1930, Hayashi had been a member of the then active Proletarian Literature Movement, but on its suppression by the Special Higher Police and a successful brainwashing of many left wing intellectuals, he had turned to ultranationalism and been associated with the mid-1930s right wing literary movement called the Japanese Romantics. His use of the previously banned term 'Greater East Asia War' itself carried great impact after its recent lack of use but still more so his attempted justification of it, though in rather distinctive terms. He explained his choice of this name by his purpose, namely to convince the Japanese of their need to form their own independent understanding of the war, as distinct either from the U.S. view of it as a crusade of democracy against fascism, the Soviet view in terms of a struggle between rival but comparable imperialisms, and the Chinese perspective of a national resurgence based on resistance to Japan. He disclaimed any affiliation with either left wing or right wing groups, aiming only at the restoration of pride in Japan.

He begins by denying that, in justifying the war, he would advocate any future repetition of it. He acknowledged that there were some elements in Japan who might wish this, either in terms of a new 'punitive war' against Communist China in alliance with the United States (contemplated in Kishi's time) or a revived co-prosperity sphere based on economic cooperation in Southeast Asia. Any such possible future developments, he claimed, would be of a quite different character from the Greater East Asia War, as the historical context which had produced it had definitely passed.

This epoch had been that of Western imperialist domination of East Asia, during which time war had been so frequent, involving Japan from the war against Manchu-ruled China in 1894, that the intervening periods of peace appear as mere pauses to prepare for the next round. So Hayashi regards the wars of the century ending in 1945 as being in reality one Hundred Year War of which the Greater East Asia War was merely the culmination. He is able to date this century neatly beginning in 1845. In that year, only a few years after the Opium War had marked the first Western aggression against East Asia and amid much increased Western navigation in the waters around Japan, Commander Biddle of the United States led two warships into what is now called Tokyo Bay to demand that the Shogunate enter into diplomatic and trade relations. The force at his command was not sufficient to overawe the Shogunate and is described by Hayashi as essentially a reconnaissance force. As is well known, it was followed up by Perry's more powerful expedition in 1853 which effectively led to the end of Japan's more than two centuries of peace in isolation, with the imposition of the Five-Power Unequal Treaties in 1858.

The first military actions involving Japan were the allied bombardments in the 1860s of the western towns of Kagoshima and Shimonoseki, the centers of a movement to expel the foreigners from Japan. This latter then changed its strategy, but not its fundamental aims, by overthrowing the Shogunate and introducing a vigorous modernizing program as the only feasible means to

28

keep the West at bay and abolish the Unequal Treaties. The new imperial regime supplemented this material program by cultivating an intensely nationalistic spirit on the Western model through education and propaganda through the media. This education is blamed by pacifists for leading Japan to war, but Hayashi claims that it was not the cause of the war but a response to the Western threat, which by the end of the century had engulfed the rest of Asia. He then traces subsequent developments with ample documentation down to the Greater East Asia War which, though a defeat in the immediate sense, accomplished the historical role of triggering the collapse of the Western colonial order and concluding Japan's Hundred Year War of resistance to Western domination. He therefore regards it as historically justified by its outcome, which he argues is the only way to evaluate historical events.

> Although it appears as a war of aggression, it was in essence a war of liberation.... The great impact imparted by this 'reckless war' at this turning point in world history is attested by the course of postwar history, without need for attestation by Wells or Toynbee [world historians on the grandest scale].

The major weakness in this argument of course is that, far from resisting the West on behalf of Asia, Japan had actually followed Fukuzawa Yukichi's line of 'abandoning Asia and joining Europe' in the Anglo-Japanese Alliance and later the Washington Pact, which was designed to preserve the status quo. The 'Greater East Asia' theme was taken up only opportunistically when the Japanese authorities, in the world crisis precipitated by the Depression, concluded that Japan's continued participation in the existing world order was no longer serving the country's interests. Hayashi did, however exert, some influence on popular war literature of the time, notably a nine volume *Stories of the Pacific War* published by Kodansha over 1965 to 1971. But at the time, his line found no response in the establishment, which maintained the 'double standard' of not openly challenging the Tokyo Trial view of history while not actively inculcating it.

Towards the other end of the ideological spectrum, it was also at this time that Professor Ienaga Saburo in 1965 began his decades of litigation against distortions or concealments in the treatment of the war in school textbooks, arising from reactionary trends in the Education Ministry's screening process—a complex subject for special treatment in a later chapter.

In that same year, academic and technical studies on the war began with the establishment of the Military History Society, embracing both research staff in the Self Defense Forces and general historians. The first issue of its periodical *Military History Studies* pointed out reasonably enough that, since so much human history is occupied or affected by war, its proper understanding is an essential part of the whole picture—a somewhat apologetic approach probably only necessary in the climate of a general aversion to the idea of war pervading the nation as a whole, not least among academics. The major research effort by these circles was the *Greater East Asia War Series* of which 102 volumes were published up to 1980 by the National Institute for Defense Studies. Its title was probably not chosen for ideological reasons but rather to reflect wartime usage, particularly as 'Pacific War' is in fact too limiting.

It was based on archives and is valuable for factual data but is criticized by Professor Fujiwara Akira, a former army officer who had collaborated in the Marxist-oriented *History of Showa* (and later became active in Professor Ienaga's campaign), on three main grounds. First, accounts concentrated on combat operations to the neglect of problems of communications and supply. Second, wartime rivalry between army and navy had carried over, so that volumes by writers in one service are critically biased against the other. Third, there is no fundamental reflection on the nature of the war, if anything there is a tendency to apologetics. Any consideration of the forces' fatal politicization is omitted.

In late 1970, there occurred a singularly traumatic episode, reminiscent of the turmoil of the 1930s, which for a time triggered intense debate on the contemporary state of the Japanese national psyche, though without any long-term effects beyond a limited cult circle. It was precipitated by the leading writer Mishima Yukio. Like Hayashi Fusao, he had had an early association with the Japanese Romantics, but in the immediate postwar period, when their vision of an idealized cultural nationalism was generally felt to be irrelevant, he achieved considerable success in depicting its obverse in abnormal psychology and social dislocation on the contemporary scene.

Later, however, he reverted to romantic nationalist themes, glorifying the tragic heroes of the failed 1936 coup and other right wing radicals of the period, with a mystical treatment of wartime sacrifices. He also produced extensive essays on the 'logic of action' and 'cultural self-defense,' represented as the most fundamental prerequisite of any other form of defense. In the mid-1960s, he organized nearly a hundred right wing students into the Shield Society, a name implying that its aim was to defend the Emperor and the Japanese spirit from the prevalent decadence of society and the corrupting influence of both the conservative regime and the left wing.

He arranged for this group to be given formal military training, usually held around the evocatively sacred peak of Mount Fuji, by the Self Defense Forces, who welcomed this as an opportunity for a good PR exercise. This was a regular concern, in view of their general lack of popularity and ambiguous constitutional status. Mishima seems to have hoped that the next wave of demonstrations against the U.S. Security Treaty might provide his group with an opportunity for heroic deeds and possibly a lever to propel constitutional revision, but, although these demonstrations, climaxing in 1969, were more violent than those of 1960, they were less purposefully directed and disintegrated in factional conflicts.

Mishima therefore decided that the only hope for constitutional change to legitimize the armed forces and restore the Emperor to his prewar status was to incite a Tokyo garrison of the Self Defense Forces to repeat the venture of 1936. On the same day as he delivered his last dramatic manuscript to the publisher, he took a handful of his followers on what seemed one of their regular visits to the garrison headquarters, where they imprisoned the commander while Mishima summoned the troops to deliver a highly colored manifesto. He declared that he was taking this action out of love for the SDF, as the 'True Japan' no longer existed apart from them—'the only place where, in this tepid contemporary Japan, it is still possible to breathe a bracing spirit.'

According to Mishima:

> We have witnessed postwar Japan, infatuated with economic prosperity, forget its foundation as a country, lose its national spirit, neglect fundamentals for trivia, fall into temporizing hypocrisy and sink into a vacuity of the soul. Politics is devoted to varnishing over contradictions, self-preservation and lust for power, with the nation's long-term destiny entrusted to a foreign country. Our vision is that it is now only in the Self-Defense Forces that the true samurai spirit survives. (*Bungei Shunju* 1995)

Mishima claimed that the unconstitutional nature of the SDF was the supreme example of corruption and deception in Japanese life and that it was now merely an augmented police force rather than the 'true guardian of Japan's historical culture and tradition centered on the Emperor.' If it did not act, it would amount to no more than its description by the left wing— 'permanent mercenaries for America.'

And then finally: 'Is no one willing to die with us in challenging this emasculating Constitution?'

But the troops he addressed were pure professionals who had undergone little of the sort of conditioning that might have brought a response to such rhetoric from an earlier generation. So Mishima and his most devoted follower took their lives by samurai-style disembowelment (*Seppuku*), being given the *coup de grace,* as prescribed, by their companions. These last were sentenced to four years imprisonment, being treated as accomplices rather than principals. Although it is hardly possible to fathom Mishima's precise state of mind, it seems likely that he had foreseen the actual outcome, possibly in the hope that his gesture might have some political effect. But instead it obliged the establishment to reaffirm adherence to the Constitution, as any other course might encourage adventuristic challenges to it.

Memories of the China war assumed greater prominence in the following year with the publication in the *Asahi* of the series *Travels in China* by Honda Katsuichi. At this stage, the United States was still preventing Japan from normalizing relations with China, though a survey by the *Mainichi* in early

31

1970 found that 86 percent of respondents favored normalization and only 4 percent regarded it as 'unnecessary.' Of those in favor, the commonest reason given by 50 percent was that the two countries were 'neighbors of common race and culture.' The next commonest reason, given by 47 percent (with overlap) was commercial opportunity, while the next at 31 percent was a fear of falling behind the world trend towards recognizing the Chinese regime. Only 15 percent mentioned 'postwar settlement' as a motive—an index of the still persisting low awareness of China's and Asia's significance in the war.

Despite the lack of diplomatic relations, a considerable commerce had developed through companies recommended by the mediation of the Japanese Socialist Party. The Japanese Communist Party was excluded from these relations because its members had felt unable to condone the chaos and cruelties of the Cultural Revolution, which had began in 1966. The Japanese Communist Party was in turn disowned as a fraternal party by the Maoist regime as having lost the revolutionary spirit. By the early 1970s, however, disorder in China was abating and visits by sympathetic Japanese were being facilitated.

Honda, who expressed the opinion that 'to conceal a crime amounts to a second crime,' concentrated on research into the Nanking Massacre of late 1937, both collecting accounts from victims and witnesses and conducting field studies of related sites. This episode had already been notorious during the war as the 'Rape of Nanking' and had figured in the class A war trials as mentioned, but an accurate assessment of its scale and nature had not been made. The Japanese army had remained in occupation of the area until 1945 and subsequent research had been hampered by the Chinese civil war, while the Communist regime, when established, was much more pressingly concerned with current problems such as land reform and the Korean War. Although this massacre was later to become the central symbolic issue in debates on the war in China, it had not been much highlighted before Honda's pioneering work. He defined its scope as covering the whole complex of operations from the landings at Shanghai and up to the fall of the walled city of Nanking itself, rather than the last phase alone as had usually been done. He explored the whole area closely and subsequently remained an active researcher and debater on this event as it assumed prominence.

An outline of the campaign provides background for later controversy. After the Japanese seizure of Manchuria and some localized operations in the extreme north of China proper, as then known, sustained fighting began in July 1937 with clashes at the Marco Polo Bridge near Peking between Japanese troops and, ironically, those of a puppet authority set up by the Japanese themselves. There are allegations, difficult to evaluate, that these clashes were to some extent provoked by Communist agents as part of a strategy to seize power by fomenting a war of resistance against Japan, but it is at least clear that the recently formed united front between Nationalists and Communists had so far stiffened national resolve that conflict could not be restricted to a piecemeal scale. Fighting spread to Shanghai around the foreign settlements and the Japanese government dispatched an expeditionary force under General Matsui Iwane (ultimately to be one of those executed as a class A war criminal), who was expected to be able to handle the situation there.

As he was not on the active list and had to be called up from the reserve, it appears that the high command did not expect the campaign to assume greater importance than the earlier localized clashes. The government was giving top priority to the Soviet Frontier with Manchukuo, where indeed major clashes occurred over the next two years, and all-out war was long considered possible. At Shanghai, however, Chinese resistance was so effective, being sustained by the hope that the Western colonial powers would intervene, that the Japanese government found it necessary to dispatch another force to land at Hangchou Bay to achieve a breakthrough at Shanghai. General Matsui was placed in command of the combined forces.

It was mid-November before the whole Shanghai area was secured, and, as the Chinese continued to resist, the Japanese maintained their drive in the direction of the capital Nanking. Matsui appears to have outrun General Staff instructions in the hope that he could distinguish himself by taking the capital and ending the war with the momentum of his troops' current advance—one of the many cases in that period of subordinates getting out of control. The General Staff only authorized an attack on Nanking at the beginning of December.

This caused special problems because adequate arrangements for supply had not been made nor were the troops relieved or rotated as would have been normal in a properly conducted campaign. Most of them, like Matsui himself, had been reservists, following normal occupations and having to leave their families and other responsibilities when called upon to leave for what was expected to be a brief emergency that would not last beyond the summer. Now, as the season grew colder and they lacked suitable winter equipment, the intense exasperation that would more rationally be directed towards the troops' superiors could only be vented on the Chinese, blamed for stubbornly prolonging their hardships. This added a sharper edge to the action each unit was authorized to take to 'requisition supplies' from the local populace. When these resisted, the fury and violence of the Japanese intensified. As winter arrived, quite cold for the latitude because of the continental air mass, the troops took shelter in houses from which the occupants were ejected—sometimes killed out of fear that they might take vengeance during the night. As tends to happen in such situations, rapes were frequent, and, as rape was forbidden and the military police (*Kempeitai* in their primary function) were known to shoot offenders out of hand, it was common to kill the victims and witnesses to prevent the crime becoming known. On occasions when there were casualties among foraging parties due to Chinese resistance, a whole neighborhood might be massacred and burned out.

A week into December, Nanking was encircled from the land side. The final target was the historic walled city, though this only occupied a small part of the whole urban area, which had a population of slightly over one million. On the one hand, the Japanese hoped that the capital's fall, accompanied by a display of ruthlessness, would suffice to end Chinese resistance, while on the other hand, the Chinese government had already resolved to continue resistance inland and to treat Nanking as an expendable pawn, useful only to delay the Japanese advance as long as possible. In accordance with this strategy, the most effective troops were withdrawn for future use, leaving the defense of Nanking to hastily recruited irregulars. These are estimated to have numbered 150,000. Any retreat by these troops was prevented by the Chinese command destroying or concealing any boats that could be used for the only open escape route across the Yangtze River.

All but 20 or so of the foreign residents, as well as Chinese elite, living in the embassy and academic quarter had already evacuated it, leaving it to be declared an international safety zone for refugees who poured in from the suburbs as the Japanese advanced. Most of the ordinary residents of the walled city not called to military duty remained in their homes. On 12 December, the Chinese commander, judging further resistance to be pointless, withdrew from the city with his senior staff and followed the government officials who had earlier left to move via Hankow to the wartime fortress of Chungking. It is sometimes suggested that at this stage, a formal surrender of the city would not have harmed subsequent Chinese resistance inland and might have avoided the worst excesses that followed, but no definite instructions reached the defending forces. These fell into complete disorder, some continuing localized resistance, some surrendering, and some changing into plain clothes, hoping to escape identification as troops.

The Japanese forces occupied the walled city the next day and were ordered to extirpate any sign of resistance in time for an orderly entry by General Matsui on 17 December. This meant massacring all surviving Chinese troops, whether captured, surrendered, or attempting to escape, including many who tried to cross the Yangtze on rafts or logs, who were also attacked from the air. Civilians suspected of being deserters were also killed, sometimes because their hands were seen to be not those of common laborers. After all sign of resistance was quelled, the troops celebrated with an orgy of rape and pillaging of treasures which they hoped (again vainly) soon to be able to take home to Japan. Arson was used to destroy evidence of such crimes. The international safety zone was largely respected, though apparently searched for deserters, and remaining foreign residents gathered some evidence of the fate of the rest of the city.

The Japanese command appear to have regretted the scale of excesses committed, one sign of this being the inauguration in this area of the system of 'comfort women,' a combination of professional and coerced prostitution to provide a sexual outlet for troops as a precaution against further mass rapes. In the following February, General Matsui invited the leading members of the International Safety Zone Committee to his headquarters and in the course of a speech to them expressed apology for 'a number of dishonorable acts' committed by Japanese troops. Order was completely restored only with the establishment of a puppet Chinese administration in March, to which the Japanese had to impart credibility for their own purposes.

A good deal of information on all aspects of this campaign was contained in Honda's accounts, and these, together with other sources, seem to have had some impact on public opinion judging by the contrast in two surveys conducted in June 1967 and April 1972. In the former, only 17 percent of respondents considered the war in China to have been wrong, while 10 percent considered it proper and 36 percent unavoidable. In the second, the first category had risen to 26 percent, while the second had dropped to 8 percent, though the third had risen to 47 percent, the first and third having absorbed some of the large noncommitted response in the earlier survey. Either way, the results indicated a greater public awareness of China arising from the current intensive debate on the question of normalizing diplomatic relations with China.

In the previous October, China had been admitted to the United Nations despite continued U.S. opposition, and in February, President Nixon, as part of a new global strategy, visited China and issued a joint statement of intent to normalize relations, though this was delayed for some years by the Vietnam War. Meanwhile, in July, a change of government in Japan had brought a break in the dominance of the 'Yoshida school' with the accession to Prime Minister of Tanaka Kakuei, a purely professional politician of humble provincial background. Though outside the dominant bureaucratic-academic network, he displayed a rare genius for manipulating the LDP's factional struggles, with covert support by underground and right wing elements and fueled by corruption raised to an unprecedented level.

This became clear only later, however, and for the moment, he achieved popularity by boldly moving to open formal relations with China, normalized in September. The Chinese did not demand reparations as such, but substantial economic aid was assured, and for a long time afterwards they refrained from raising issues of war guilt or even any reminders or commemoration of the Nanking Massacre. They were not yet disposed to dispute Tanaka's reply, when questioned by a Communist Diet member whether the war in China was plainly aggression, to the effect that this was 'something to be evaluated by future historians.'

3 Oil shock and restabilization (1973-1981)

This period was transitional in various respects. During this time, the proportion of the Japanese population born since the war came to form a majority. Among other effects, this meant that the generation that had grown up in the atmosphere of postwar civil society would tend to feel remote from the cruder jingoism of an earlier generation and, though still at times fascinated by the war over the growing distance of time, was bound to form new perspectives more relevant to the contemporary outlook.

At the same time, the Cold War had developed a more inertial character as compared with its earlier intensity, though the basic alignments persisted and were for a time reactivated by the 'New Cold War' resulting from the Soviet invasion of Afghanistan in 1979, before finally giving way to fluidity as the 1980s progressed.

On the domestic scene, Prime Minister Tanaka enjoyed some additional early popularity from initiatives to correct the problems and dislocations resulting from the preceding period of all-out economic growth, but the whole economy and society was by then badly hit by the 'oil-shock' of late 1973. The massive rise in oil prices arising from the Middle Eastern war of that year brought growth to an abrupt halt and demanded drastic restructuring.

Then, during the following year, Tanaka's intricate empire of corruption was revealed, most decisively by a devastatingly thorough *expose* in the *Bungei Shunju* in November, detailing the damning results of months of full-time investigation by a team of 20 specialists. Tanaka resigned shortly afterwards amid turmoil in the Diet and later was found to be implicated in an even more massive scandal involving the Lockheed Corporation. An intermediary role had been played by a veteran right wing figure, previously much admired in kindred circles. Disillusionment caused one of Mishima's young idealists to attempt his assassination at the cost of his own life by crashing a hired light airplane into his home, though the intended victim escaped.

Tanaka's machine continued to manipulate LDP politics, but after his resignation, formal power reverted to the bureaucratic 'Yoshida School.' Yet the party's hold on government became precarious and from 1976 to 1980, it lost control of the Upper House. During the same period, local government in the larger cities was dominated by left wing administrations which in Tokyo dated from 1967. This was to some extent a reaction against the central government's domination by the LDP's mainly rural base, which through malapportionment kept it in power with less than a majority vote. Japanese management, however, showed remarkable adaptability in recovering from the oil shock without major social disruption and was so much more successful in this than other major economies that Japan came to be generally viewed both at home and abroad as an 'economic superpower' and 'Number One' in management skills. This in turn led to more optimistic appraisals by Japanese of their society and culture, which included some more positive evaluations of the legacy of the wartime experience as contributing to Japan's postwar success. Some substance in this approach has also been recognized by such an able American authority as John W. Dower, who, in his *Japan in War and Peace* (New Press, New York 1995), speaks of 'the useful war' in this sense.

In Japan, this trend took the form of a 'businessman's war literature,' meaning studies of the war from the standpoint of its lessons for management, either positive or negative. Something of this approach had been pioneered much earlier in Kurita Industries, established by a former naval lieutenant who was a graduate of the Naval Engineering College. He had described company staff by a military type term for 'recruits' and called his departments 'units,' with a command structure appropriate to such concepts. This line of thought took on an ideological flavor in the 1970s when the nature of 'Japanese-style management' was being actively refined in conjunction with the process of restructuring after the oil shock.

This vogue was heralded by the publication by a former lieutenant-colonel in 1972 of a wartime policy document *Principles of Command*, presented as a text for 'strategic management.' Next came the two volume *Financiers' Pacific War Records*, published over 1973-74 by the *Bungei Shunju*, containing accounts of both the wartime experiences of successful businessmen and the manner in which they had applied the lessons then learned to their postwar enterprises.

In the late 1970s, this treatment was taken up on a regular basis by an established monthly journal for businessmen called *President*, which pursued studies of wars over a wide range of periods and places by way of deriving lessons for contemporary management. A 1978 special issue of studies in 'naval style management' stated that: 'contemporary enterprises can learn a great deal from "naval style management" in principles of organization, personnel control and training systems.... The navy was the precursor of modern management techniques in Japan.' Other such special issues carried such observations as: 'there are many instructive suggestions for businessmen in the achievements of Admiral Yamamoto' [architect of the Pearl Harbor attack and other noteworthy exploits]. 'Valuable lessons applicable to contemporary business society are latent in the naval defeat at Midway' [first major turning point in the war at sea]. 'The imperial army suffered from the "large enterprise disease."'

This last is an example of a growing bias favoring the navy as being, from the contemporary viewpoint, more liberal in outlook and rational in procedure as compared with the army's image of feudal high-handedness and premodern overreliance on psychological factors and morale. As with popular images of any kind, these distinctions were not wholly authentic. It was true that Navy Ministry circles had shown a more cautious attitude in the years leading up to the war and had been regarded by the Emperor's advisors as a force for moderation as against army impetuosity, but the Naval General Staff was more aggressively inclined. As regards liberalism, naval distinctions of rank were even more extreme than the army's. One perhaps significant example is the 'comfort women' system, where in the army's case all ranks generally used the same facility at different hours, while the navy had separate facilities for officers and other ranks with the more attractive women being reserved for the exclusive use of the naval officers. But there was enough substance in the stereotypes to ensure a growing appeal by the navy for the new generation, combined with the social influence of certain former navy elements.

One particular category of ex-naval staff who figured conspicuously in key fields had served in the 'short term active service navy paymaster' program, being selected from among new tertiary graduates and after special training appointed for a two-year term of duty as paymaster officers. Men of this background were widely noted later as occupying key positions in finance, bureaucracy, and politics. A parallel group, with background in the Naval Technical Research Institute, particularly relating to wartime radar research, was regarded as having formed the nucleus for Japan's later spectacular success in electronics. A significant factor was, of course, that the death rate in the accounting and technical arms had been much lower than for those in the combat service from their being mainly stationed in base areas or having shorter tours of duty.

Evidence of ex-navy influence at the highest political level was provided by the formation of a Diet members' 'Old Navy Club' in April 1978, comprising 47 members from both houses and all parties except the Communists. In their inaugural meeting they wore field officers' service caps, saluted the naval ensign to a bugle call, observed silent prayers for the fallen, and practiced naval songs. Among them was Nakasone Yasuhiro, of naval paymaster background, who was later as Prime Minister to be involved in controversy about Japan's attitude toward the war.

At another level from business or political circles, the same period saw a vogue of literature dealing with wartime experience on the home front, sometimes promoted by local administrations in the interest of preserving local history. A leader here was the island of Okinawa, which the United States had agreed in 1971 to return to Japanese sovereignty the following year, though with the retention of military bases much larger than elsewhere in Japan. Okinawa was the only part of the Japanese homeland to have suffered land warfare and that on a most devastating scale, in which something like a quarter of the population perished—some at the hands of the Japanese forces themselves, a subject of later controversy. A volume of the Okinawa Prefectural History published in 1971 dealt with the battle of Okinawa and was followed by another in 1975. The main sources were symposia held in all parts of the Ryukyu Islands and combined many hundreds of personal recollections. The compiler criticized earlier accounts of the battle as portraying the islanders' role as one of heroic self-sacrifice in the nation's defense and sought to balance such a perspective by a realistic portrayal of their life under wartime conditions and the Japanese army's treatment of them as expendable.

Okinawans and Ryukyuans generally have, at any time, been treated as second-class subjects and were in prewar times described as constituting a 'quasi-external territory' because Ryukyu was only annexed in modern times after a long and independent history as a maritime kingdom. Their dialect is quite unintelligible to other Japanese, though related, and their physical build and subtropical lifestyle are distinctive.

The rest of Japan, though spared land combat by an imperial decision too late to save Okinawa, had been subject to devastating air raids on most important cities, including the atomic bombing of Hiroshima and Nagasaki. These latter cases, because of their distinctive and rather symbolic character for a postwar world living under the threat of nuclear war, had been extensively studied from an earlier stage, but from the 1970s compilations of popular experience under bombing came to be undertaken systematically in all areas. The pioneer volume was *Tokyo's Great Air Raids* of 1971, and other studies conducted by local societies, formed for the purpose, continued over the following years. The results were consolidated in a ten volume *Japan's Air Raids* published over 1980-81.

Such studies were welcomed as something quite new in depicting the life of the common people under wartime conditions, in contrast to the exclusive concentration hitherto on military or political figures. A particular novelty was that for the first time they included the experiences of women, hitherto neglected but actually fulfilling a vital role in maintaining society and industry while most of the male population were diverted elsewhere. The continuing Vietnam War was also initially a stimulus to recreating wartime memories, both because of the unparalleled intensity of the bombing over several years and the fact that bases in Okinawa were used for this purpose.

Another massive project along parallel lines was undertaken by the Buddhist lay organization Soka Gakkai (Value-creating Society) which has always been strongly antimilitarist because of the persecution suffered by its founders under the wartime regime because they placed Buddhism above the State Shinto cult. Buddhists were tolerated so long as they did not challenge the state cult openly, but the Soka Gakkai's first founder refused to compromise and died in prison. The political party later founded by this society, the Komeito (Clean Government Party), became the second largest opposition party in the Diet and consistently opposed constitutional revision. In 1974, the general conference of its youth department took up a program of activities called the 'Youth Department's appeal for the protection of the Peace Constitution.' Part of this was a compilation of the wartime experiences of the society's members, and, as there were many millions of these, a great deal of material was assembled. The results were published under the title *To the Generation who did not know the War* in two series, one of 56 volumes published over 1974-79 and a later series of 24 volumes over 1981-85.

Still another such project but with a regional basis was the *Yomiuri* series *War,* covering personal experience over the Fifteen Year War—a new alternative term for the war reckoned as beginning from the Manchurian incident—in the Osaka area, published in 20 volumes over 1976-84. The central figure in this project describes it in the following terms:

> There would be no reason for *War* to exist as an official history. It is subjective, sentimental, impressionistic.... For countless people, the war is a scar that will never vanish. In a certain sense, I am probing and touching scars that it may not be desired that they be touched. But I wish that by licking the wounds I may relieve the pain a little. Above all I feel it is important to convey the pain. As it is such an emotional undertaking, sentiment and subjectivity take precedence over logic and objectivity. (Yoshida 1995)

In this context, he was contrasting *War* with a more formal historical series, *The Emperor in Showa History,* described as 'logical, objective and factual,' which the *Yomiuri* had serialized from 1967 to 1975. It was based on direct interviews with former military figures, bureaucrats, and palace staff who had occupied key positions over the Fifteen Year War period. The completion of this series roughly coincided with the publication of two other studies of the Emperor's role—a more favorable *The Emperor* by Kojima Noboru in 1974 and a more critical *The Emperor's War Responsibility* by Inoue Kiyoshi in 1975. These were based on diaries of wartime leaders and other records becoming available over recent years. Although slanted differently, both recognized that the Emperor had been better informed about the progress of the war and more active in consultation about it than had generally been assumed in the past—ultimately the result of the 'bargain' struck on this question between the Occupation and the Japanese establishment.

Inoue's studies had originally been stimulated by the reception accorded the Emperor on his visit to Europe in 1971. Although, as an ally in the Cold War, he was warmly received at the official level—in Britain being reinstated (after the title was revoked during the war) as Knight of the Garter—there were clear signs of resentment at the popular level. This was most conspicuous in Holland but also quite marked in Denmark, Britain, and Germany, where anti-Nazi demonstrators viewed him as Hitler's wartime ally. In 1975, he visited the United States where, at a reception given by President Ford, he spoke of 'that most unfortunate war, which I deeply deplore.' This was welcomed in the United States as amounting to an apology and in fact was the closest he ever came to a formal one. A right wing apologist explains his unwillingness to apologize as stemming from concern for Japan's wartime Asian allies or collaborators, such as Wang Ching-wei, head of the client regime in Nanking from 1940, or Subhas Chandra Bose, head of the 'provisional free India government' in Singapore. The Emperor had apologized to such allies in his surrender rescript. Many had of course been executed but some had survived and become active in postwar independent regimes, as in Indonesia, Burma, Thailand, and the Philippines, in some cases restored by the Cold War as the Japanese establishment itself had been.

On the Emperor's return to Japan from the United States on this occasion, the matter of his war responsibility was taken up in a press interview, where he responded: 'As for the subtle nuances of my remark [in Washington], not being a specialist in things literary, I am afraid they are beyond me. I am not really able to respond to your question.'

Debates on his war responsibility, however, were subsequently overshadowed by other issues relating to the war, particularly as the Cold War wound down during the 1980s, until they were revived during his last illness and after his death in early 1989.

4 From the textbook uproar through the Emperor's death (1982-1990)

In July 1982, the treatment of the war in school education exploded into a major political uproar both domestically and internationally. As will be described more fully later, this issue had long been a matter of deep concern in educational circles, notably in relation to Professor Ienaga's litigation against the Education Ministry.

Under the initial occupation reforms, educational policy had been entrusted to autonomous and locally elected school boards, with the formerly all-powerful Education Ministry reduced to being a resource center for curriculum development, issuing 'draft guidelines' which school boards and teachers could apply as they saw fit. But under the 'reverse course,' the Ministry's powers were expanded, mainly by way of authority to screen textbooks for use in schools. The school boards became appointive on a local basis, while remaining administratively independent of the Ministry and entrusted with the final selection of texts for their respective areas from among the range of samples that had been authorized after screening.

Texts with a certain level of real or perceived flaws were occasionally disqualified, but most were given 'conditional qualification,' subject to attention being given to two categories of comments made by the Ministry's examiners. The first category consisted of mandatory 'corrections' of erroneous facts or figures, sometimes extended to points in dispute not thought suitable for inclusion at the relevant level of education. The other category, not binding, consisted of 'suggested improvements.' These favored neutral or 'objective' terms over emotive ones, sometimes with a leaning to euphemism. Some scope was allowed for negotiation with authors and publishers, but persistent tensions developed between the Ministry and the strongly left-leaning Japan Teacher's Union, strongly backed by the Federation of Publishing Employees' Unions. The Ministry was also subject to pressure on the other side from a cohesive grouping of education policy specialists among the ruling party's Diet members who were determined to combat leftist tendencies in education. During the later 1970s, as mentioned, the LDP was in a rather precarious position, and pressures from this direction died down. But in 1980, the party made a strong electoral recovery and its education policy group began a campaign of criticism against 'bias' in textbooks, both through the party organ *Liberal News* and by moves in the Diet for legislation to strengthen screening procedures. In reply, textbook authors in the social studies field, which included history and politics, formed a Social Studies Textbook Authors Forum as a focus for counter-lobbying.

The expansion of such issues to the international scene began on 16 June 1982, when the Education Ministry delivered to its press club, the customary PR outlet for government agencies, a sample each of 593 elementary and high school texts in all fields, screened and authorized over the previous year, from which the school boards would make selections for the following year's courses. As was customary, the journalists divided the task of examining them among the 16 newspaper and TV companies represented in the club, later sharing their findings among themselves.

As the prescreened manuscripts were retained by the Ministry and not available for inspection, it was only possible to assess the detailed effects of the screening process by contacting authors or publishers, a very extensive undertaking. The leading newspapers, however, formed the impression that Ministry policy had taken a reactionary turn and ten days later the three leading newspapers, *Asahi, Mainichi,* and *Yomiuri* attacked the screening process under headlines like: 'Further move back to "prewar" authority over textbooks.... Description of "aggression" weakened' (*Asahi*) and 'Textbook control further toughened.... "Aggression" in China to "advance"' (*Mainichi*). Even the more conservative *Sankei* followed suit the next day.

The *Asahi* listed 14 samples of undesirable screening alterations in various subjects, including the one (also occurring in the other major newspapers) that was to cause major international repercussions. This was the allegation that in a particular history textbook, the Ministry had enforced alteration of the phrases 'aggression in North China' to 'advance into North China' and 'all-out aggression against China' to 'all-out attack on China.' The press had obtained these points not directly but from a Japan TV report based on an interview with the author which was, however, misunderstood. An *Asahi* journalist had tried to check with the author and publisher, but it was only after the publication of the report that the author made it clear that his text had not in fact been altered. Another aspect that tended to be misrepresented was that amendments of this kind when made were not of the mandatory 'correction' category, but the 'suggestion' category which was not enforceable if the authors or publishers persisted. Professor Ienaga had in fact refused to change 'aggression' to 'armed advance' in a text of his which was nevertheless passed, though he objected to the informal pressure exerted on him. Many other authors of course had not resisted, even though legally able to do so, for economic or other reasons to be discussed in detail in a later chapter.

The initial reports were conveyed to China by the Xinhua press agency, but there was no reaction until 20 July, when the authorities decided to utilize them for political leverage. On that day, the LDP's special Council for Economic Policy arrived in the Taiwanese capital after a tour of Southeast Asia. Following Japan's severance of diplomatic relations with the Taiwan regime consequent on Japan's recognition of the Communist regime, contacts were maintained less formally by semiofficial means of this kind, roughly the obverse of the situation prevailing before the transfer of recognition. This visit to Taiwan, combined with current U.S. negotiations on arms sales there, strengthened hard-line accusations within China that the reformist regime of Deng Xiaoping was being too soft on Taiwanese issues, so Deng's group seized upon the textbook question as a diversion and demonstration of toughness on Japan.

For the next couple of months, the Chinese press attacked the reported alterations as a sign of revived militarism in Japan, and there was enough latent resentment of Japan, both over its wartime invasion and its Cold War role, to stimulate vigorous reactions throughout Chinese society. The suddenness of this revival of wartime issues is indicated by an experience related by Ienaga's supporter Fujiwara Akira. On 18 September the previous year, the 50th anniversary of the fabricated incident in Mukden that launched the Manchurian Incident and thus the whole Fifteen Year War, he had visited the spot but found that no commemoration of the event was being made nor was it mentioned in the Chinese press. But when the textbook issue was taken up, the Chinese revived the memory of the Nanking Massacre in particular and sought out survivors and witnesses to testify publicly about it in support of the textbook campaign. This led to the establishment of the Nanking Massacre Memorial Museum a couple of years later and a new prominence to research and debate on the subject in both China and Japan. It is suggested that one reason for the Communist regime's long silence on the massacre was that its official war history concentrated on the Communist-led guerrilla war in the north but that, since that phase of the war, though important, was diffuse and lacked any central focus, the massacre was revived as a major symbolic theme for the war of resistance. Japanese right wing revisionists and occasionally government politicians go further than this to assert that its late revival as an issue demonstrated that the massacre, at least on the scale claimed, was a fabrication. But this relates to a later period.

Once China had taken up the textbook issue so seriously, it spread like wildfire among all areas affected by the war. The inhibitions against such action resulting from the Cold War were now much diminished. The Cold War alignment itself was in decay, the Vietnam War was long over, most local insurgencies had subsided and Japanese economic aid was rather less urgently needed, though on the other hand diplomatic pressure might be useful in this respect as well.

Regarding Chinese-speaking areas alone, a researcher in the Chinese University of Hong Kong, T'an Ju-ch'ien, published a collection of source material on the 'Anti-Japanese History Revision Movement' over late July to September 1982 in China, Taiwan, and Hong Kong. It included background analysis, accounts of protest activities such as religious action and trade boycotts, music, films, TV programs and displays, together with over 200 documents such as statements by organizations, newspaper editorials, individual speeches, research, reference material, and poetry. Over 400 academics had signed statements with their blood, as did 2,000 others.

Outside these three areas, newspaper reports on the issue numbered: 145 in Macao, 946 in South Korea, 33 in North Korea, 37 in the Philippines, 75 in Indonesia, 43 in Malaysia, 312 in Singapore, 5 in Vietnam, 72 in Thailand, 24 in Burma, 19 in India, 7 in Sri Lanka, 16 in Pakistan, 12 in Bangladesh, and 16 in Australia. The large number in South Korea, which also saw mass demonstrations, boycotts, and threats to diplomatic relations, reflected the continuing deep resentments of Japan's colonial record there. One feature of reported textbook wording that especially enraged Koreans was the description of the abortive uprising of 1919, a heroic episode to them, as 'riots.' Some Koreans are offended by the term 'Fifteen Year War' because it excludes their own struggle for independence, which they represent as a state of war beginning from annexation in 1910. During most of this time, resistance was necessarily restricted to sporadic acts of what governing authorities described as 'terrorism,' including an attempt on the Emperor himself, and it was only in the late 1930s that Koreans were able to participate in guerrilla type operations in association with the Chinese Communists or in Manchuria with Soviet backing. Among the other areas mentioned, the next largest figure, given for Singapore, reflected the wartime massacres which here had affected an exceptionally large proportion of the population.

Attempted Japanese explanations to the Chinese and Koreans in terms of the actual misreporting that had occurred were not accepted, so cabinet chief secretary Miyazawa Kiichi on 26 August issued an official statement to the effect that:

> We are profoundly aware of the great suffering and loss which the actions of our country have inflicted on the nations of Asia, including Korea and China.... With a view to promoting friendship and amity with our neighbor countries in Asia we will give good heed to these criticisms and rectify matters which are the government's responsibility. (Tawara 1995)

He even added that 'the opinion of surrounding countries will be considered in future textbooks'—a suggestion that infuriated conservatives as being 'treasonable.' The idea of some sort of international commission on history textbooks has been raised in opposing quarters, but the difficulty of obtaining a consensus on historical interpretation among both Koreas, both Chinas, and Southeast Asian countries has been too obvious for this to develop far. Even some Korean members of a Japan-South Korea History Textbook Research Society, amid various frank exchanges, conceded that a formal arrangement would encroach too far on normal principles of national sovereignty. In South Korea itself there is only one prescribed history textbook prepared by the government directly—not to speak of the situation in North Korea or China!

Miyazawa made this statement essentially to facilitate the previously agreed visit to Beijing of Prime Minister Suzuki to mark the tenth anniversary of normalization. China and South Korea both accepted his statement as concluding the matter, though even then much of Suzuki's visit was spent discussing textbooks and reassuring Chinese leaders that Japan was not reverting to militarism.

The government, however, did convey the same message to the Education Ministry regarding its future policy. The Ministry had at the outset of the controversy pointed out that, even regarding alterations that had been accurately reported, there had been no change in policy, as authors and publishers in the past had often accepted similar 'suggestions' for revision. Soon afterwards, however, a leaked internal policy document on screening did indicate a preference for standardizing a suitable term to use for 'invasion.' When the Foreign Ministry reinforced Miyazawa's requirement for a more cautious future policy, the Ministry at first resisted, stiffened by the conservative Dietmen's education policy group, but protests from within the Ministry forced acceptance of the desired policy orientation, though demands from authors to provide errata to reverse some alterations were not met. The Minister, however, issued a statement to the effect that: 'Necessary consideration will be given, from the standpoint of international understanding and accord, to the treatment of modern and contemporary historical phenomena relating to neighboring Asian countries.' (Tawara 1995).

He included an exhortation to teachers that: 'it is expected that, in the teaching environment also, still more consideration will be given in future to cultivating a spirit of international understanding and accord in relation to Asian countries, especially neighboring countries.' This last point was resented by some as trying to shift responsibility to teachers who, as noted, had tended to attack the Ministry's attitude in textbook screening. Further developments in education policy will be described later.

Despite the official settlement of the issue at the international level, heated debate continued among the Japanese public and media. Right wing publications attacked the 'irresponsibility' of the popular press, and on 7 September 1982, the *Sankei*, under the headline 'We apologize deeply to our readers,' published an apology to the effect that: 'as China protested on the basis of a false report, the protest had no basis. We deeply regret our involvement in a report that created a diplomatic furor.' Other newspapers, however, were less apologetic and some tried to expel *Sankei* reporters from the Ministry's press

46

club. The *Asahi,* even though admitting error in the particular case in question, in the same issue reviewed cases of comparable alterations made at the instance of the Ministry over the past 30 years. It followed this up in later issues on the basis of alterations recorded by the Publishing Employees' Union, which in an issue of late September supplied 45 comparisons of manuscripts with screened sample texts, appearing under the heading 'tracing widespread weakening of "aggression."'

One of these was an alteration from 'control of North China' to 'advance into North China,' which was regarded as approximating the phrases at the center of the recent uproar. Besides, among the original sample texts of 16 June, there was a case where the precise alteration alleged had been made, though not with reference to China. It related to the Japanese move into southern French Indochina in mid-1941 with the agreement of the French Vichy government set up after France's defeat by Germany. The manuscript had read: 'This aggression in Southeast Asia was aimed at acquiring resources such as oil, tin, rubber and rice, resulting in a head-on clash with British, American and Dutch interests.' The text had been altered from 'aggression' to 'advance' on the basis that the French authorities had consented and no armed attack was involved. The Vietnamese government, for its part in the protest movement, had raised this point but, not carrying weight comparable to China and Korea, received little attention.

Other commentators blamed the whole embarrassment on the manner in which the Ministry conducted screening in secret and released a great number of texts at once, making accurate assessment of the position extremely difficult. But the long-term effects of the episode were much wider, as they led to a persistent tendency among many Asian countries to raise unresolved wartime issues on every possible occasion, which in turn would be backed by left wing or pacifistic elements in Japan for their basic purpose of opposition to constitutional revision. Subsequent governments were held to a conciliatory posture by financial interests, who were becoming steadily more involved in trade and investment in Asia as compared with the earlier primacy of relations with the Western camp and were well aware of the need to avoid needless provocations.

In the aftermath of the textbook uproar, the Foreign Ministry in the following year specifically informed South Korea that, in the texts issued that year, of 19 specific amendments demanded by South Korea, seven had been complied with. In 1984 it reported that eight of the other points had been revised and subsequently maintained a vigilant and generally defensive posture whenever such irritations arose. As one leading politician later put it in relation to Japan's increasing post-Cold War involvement in the Asia-Pacific region:

> Japan is a member of the Asia-Pacific region and needless to say this is the region to be most emphasized in Japan's diplomacy.... But at the

47

same time in that region distrust and caution are directed towards Japan arising from historical memories. On the political side, as Japan pursues diplomacy emphasizing the Asia-Pacific region, the historical question cannot be avoided for securing trust by the region as its point of departure.... As one aspect of past history, it will not do to deny the fact that Japan once became an aggressor in that region. (Yoshida 1995)

Despite this overall policy direction however, the contrary rise of revivalist nationalism and right wing revisionism from time to time brought embarrassments in the form of indiscreet remarks by high-ranking political figures and, although quick action was usually taken to counter these, the trend by no means subsided, as will be seen in discussing later developments.

Unit 731

A concurrent development that probably contributed to the intensity of the textbook uproar was the final comprehensive and detailed revelation of the record of the biological experimentation project usually called Unit 731, which now reached a very wide audience both in Japan and abroad. As mentioned earlier, although occupation intelligence became aware of the Unit's nature quite soon after the end of the war, its members were spared prosecution in exchange for their data and assistance to U.S. biological warfare research. Many of them later pursued successful careers in medicine and research institutions, including professorships at major universities.

Some fragmentary knowledge of the unit's activities did, however, surface from time to time before its major exposure in the early 1980s. The basic U.S. policy was already decided by the end of 1945 with the preliminary investigation by Colonel Murray Sanders, though a full-scale study of Unit 731, followed by final policy decisions, was only completed about mid-1947 with the more expert investigations by Dr Norbert Fell of the U.S. Chemical Warfare Service. Meanwhile, however, in January 1946 the occupation newspaper *Stars and Stripes* carried a relevant report from Communist informants who in the earliest phase of the occupation had welcomed Allied forces as 'liberators' and naturally enough cooperated in the initial exposure and suppression of militaristic and ultranationalistic elements.

According to the Communist sources, Lieutenant General Ishii Shiro, the top commanding officer of Unit 731, had directed human biological warfare experiments on both Chinese and American prisoners in Manchuria. Although Ishii's name was already known to intelligence from earlier contacts with his former subordinates, it was only after this report appeared that he was located and taken into what amounted to protective custody quite separately from war criminal suspects, partly to avoid the risk of any leak to Soviet intelligence and partly to avoid any involvement with war crimes proceedings. Occupation censorship allowed no scope for questions to be raised in the Japanese press, which merely reported that Ishii was 'to be questioned on technical matters of medical treatment.'

The matter of Unit 731 became public briefly at the end of 1949 when the Soviet authorities conducted a trial in Khabarovsk, Siberia, of 12 of the unit's members whom they had captured in the swift advance into Manchuria in the last week of the war. The trial lasted only six days, taking the usual Soviet pattern of full confessions by all accused with pleas for lenience. There were no executions, though the evidence presented would have justified this on the basis adopted in class Band C cases tried by the other allies. Prison terms ranged from two to 25 years, though all were actually repatriated to Japan by 1956, and it is speculated that here too some degree of lenience may have been given in exchange for data and cooperation.

The evidence presented was generally accurate in the light of later revelations and was startling enough to be reported in some Western media, including the *New York Times*. The prosecution's summing up had included demands for the trial of Ishii and others responsible, including the Emperor, all of whom the United States was accused of protecting. These demands were followed by diplomatic approaches early in the following year, as well as a summary of the trial proceedings in book form by the Soviet Foreign Language Publishing House. Occupation GHQ, however, following directions from the U.S. State Department, denied that it held any information on such biological experiments, and claimed that the timing of the trials indicated a propagandist aim, designed to counter current agitation concerning the fate of 376,000 Japanese prisoners and internees captured by the Soviet Union in Manchuria and unaccounted for. Those who had survived were being held as slave labor for postwar reconstruction projects, more or less in lieu of reparations, until most were repatriated during the 1950s. The Japanese press naturally followed the GHQ line, negating the effect of reports of the trials by juxtaposing them with reports of diplomatic moves relating to the prisoners in Siberia. The Communist *Red Flag* of course upheld the validity of the trials and printed interviews with four ex-soldiers who claimed personal knowledge of Unit 731. But under Cold War conditions, it was easy for both Japan and the Western camp to discount any allegations from Communist sources.

When the Korean War began a few months afterwards, the occupation issued new censorship guidelines to the media which, in addition to the normal secrecy on military activities, banned all mention of biological warfare or any epidemics among the United Nations forces. This naturally inhibited any further discussion on Unit 731 and recalls accusations, originating in the Communist camp but later treated with some seriousness by Western researchers, that the U.S. forces in the Korean War employed some of the methods developed and tested by Ishii's organization. The subject then faded from public attention for many years, the silence only broken by sporadic references in war reminiscences. Ienaga recalls having first read material on Unit 731 in a confessional piece by one of its members about ten years after the war and being shocked by it. He took up the matter in his campaign later when more information was available. Some brief impact was made in November 1976 by a TV documentary on Tokyo Broadcasting Service entitled *A Bruise—Terror of the 731 Corps*. It was the result of three years' research by its producer Ms Yoshinaga Haruko. The *Washington Post* ran a front-page story on the broadcast, but the subject then faded again from public notice.

It finally entered the mainstream of war literature with the serialization in the *Red Flag* of the results of exhaustive investigations by Morimura Seiichi under the title *The Devil's Gluttony*. The *Red Flag* had long expanded from a party organ to a very successful general interest newspaper, its revenue providing the major part of Communist Party funds. The series was also soon published in book form in three volumes, the first of which became the best seller of 1982 with sales of 1.5 million copies, just as the textbook uproar was raging. It was written in novelistic form, which doubtless added to its readability and popularity, but the context was substantially accurate and authentic. It was simultaneously supplemented by more academic and strictly factual studies by Tsuneichi Keiichi, beginning with *The Germ Warfare Unit that Disappeared* in 1981. Still further impact on Japanese perceptions came via the United States from an article in the October 1981 Issue of the *Bulletin of Atomic Scientists* by J. W. Powell, earlier a victim of the McCarthyite frenzy of the 1950s. It was entitled 'Japan's Biological Weapons: 1930-1945, a Hidden Chapter in History.' This was largely based on U.S. documentation and included an account of the cover-up. Questions in the Japanese Diet stirred by these various revelations brought the first ever government admission that Unit 731 had existed. It was also mentioned in the Diet that Ishii had been given a handsome retirement pension. He had died in 1959.

The formal title of Unit 731 was 'Headquarters, Epidemic Prevention and Water Supply Division, Kwantung Army' (the overall term for forces stationed in Manchuria). Water purification is of course a vital function for preventing epidemics in any armed force, and when this and affiliated units were referred to officially, they were assumed to be engaged only in this type of function. The nucleus of the organization, from 1933, was a 200-man water purification squad stationed near Harbin, the largely White Russian city roughly in the center of Manchuria. It was headed by Ishii, then classed as a senior medical officer. He had previously formed close links in the upper military bureaucracy in Japan and his appointment here indicates that he was expected to assume an important future role. In 1936, the squad's status was raised to that of division, with autonomy in staffing, budget, and operations. Ishii found it easy to recruit well qualified staff because, as in other fields, the puppet state of Manchukuo seemed like a land of opportunity compared with the limitations of life in Japan in the aftermath of the Depression. As Tsuneishi puts it: 'Scientists and technologists were better accommodated in Manchuria than in Japan with respect to availability of research funds and freedom

50

to select research themes. Manchuria was probably like a newly found paradise for these people.' (Harris 1994)

From that year, the unit began experiments on political prisoners arrested by the 'antisubversive' Special Service Agency and held in Harbin prison. This began with tests mainly of bubonic plague, cholera, typhus, and dysentery as the first phase in preparing for possible large-scale biological warfare later. In 1938, when it was realized that the war in China would be protracted, the division was reorganized as a separate secret unit and in 1939 shifted for security purposes to Pingfang, about 20 kilometers to the south. The local inhabitants were cleared from an area six kilometers square to form a special military zone. On this were constructed an airfield, a power plant, a branch railway line, an underground fuel depot, laboratories, a lecture hall, quarters for staff, who reached a maximum of 2,600, training facilities, a sports ground, a riding ground, and a shrine of the State Shinto cult—usual in established military units. This one was dedicated to Admiral Togo, a leading hero of the Russo-Japanese War of 1904-05—a case of the common custom of deifying exemplary historical characters. In addition, and most ominously, was a pair of prisons called 'log pens' from the custom of describing experimental subjects as 'logs,' on the analogy of logs to be cut up for timber in the same way as these were to be dissected or vivisected. A photograph of the compound is held by Morimura.

In 1940, the unit was designated 'Headquarters, Epidemic and Water Supply Division,' with the code number Unit 731. The activities pursued within it were later appropriately described as the 'secret of secrets.' Even Japanese aircraft were forbidden to fly over it, and it was supplied with a fighter plane authorized to shoot down any doing so. The staff comprised physicians, researchers, and assistants assembled from all parts of Japan and included nurses and midwives as well as 200 teenage trainees. The 300 military personnel were mainly classed as paramilitary, Ishii holding the rank of Major General, later Lieutenant General.

The staff do not appear to have been of the natural sadist type common in the Kempeitai and the Thought Police or their counterparts in other totalitarian systems but rather the type of scientists who can dedicate themselves totally to the solution of purely scientific problems in fields like biological or nuclear war, unaffected by considerations of possible effects on humanity. As Tsuneishi again puts it:

> In everyday society, there is no such distinction on reasons for killing. In the field of science, however, killing can result in new findings or a revolutionary breakthrough which would benefit all mankind. The scientist who brought about the same would naturally make quite a name for himself. (Harris 1994)

51

Ishii was also insistent on the duty of staff to serve Emperor and country. A vast variety of diseases were tested under his direction. In addition to those already mentioned were smallpox, tetanus, tuberculosis, river fever, gangrene, botulism, influenza, tick encephalitis, anthrax, leprosy, and syphilis. Local diseases little known hitherto were also studied. To the best of present knowledge, something like 3,000 'logs' died from these and other tests from 1940 to 1945. This figure is based on the record of the X-rays taken of all subjects on their introduction, with the aim of determining their initial state of health as a basis of assessing the results of later tests. When X-rayed, each was allotted a number for subsequent identification. Numbering began from 101 and on reaching 1,500 began again from 101. A member of the X-ray team who had joined it in 1942 took up numbering from a little over 100 of the second cycle and had almost reached the next 1,500 when the war ended. This means that the overall total would have approached 3,000 at least, not counting the units earlier activities from 1936.

Experiments comprised the following five main categories:

1. Infection, treatment, and prevention of epidemic diseases. Use was made of bacteria cultured by a specialized team to a virulence many times greater than normal. Plague was administered by injection, dysentery by drinking, and typhus by food, while the spread of such diseases from one 'log' to others was monitored. Venereal disease transmission, a big problem in the Japanese army as well as most others, was studied by the enforced intercourse by an infected person with one uninfected. Serum and vaccine were extracted by vivisection.

2. Development of delivery systems. The unit used fleas as carriers to propagate plague. These were infected by allowing them to suck the blood of rats injected with the bacteria and confined in oil drums, of which the unit used 4,500. The fleas were then encased in ceramic bombs which would explode at a low temperature. These were dropped from the air at a testing ground at Anda, 140 kilometers north of Harbin, around 'logs' tied naked to stakes to facilitate the sucking of their blood by the fleas. Humans were also used to test the effect of firearms and flame-throwers. Plague infection was also tested by spraying the victims indoors.

3. Frostbite. 'Logs' who had survived disease experiments were used for tests on frostbite. The winter temperature at Harbin averages -35 to -40 degrees centigrade. The victims would be placed out of doors, dressed in winter clothing but with hands and feet exposed. When they were doused with water, they immediately developed frostbite and on becoming necrotic were struck with sticks to check whether the nerves were still functioning. These limbs were then immersed in hot water of various temperatures to test the degree of muscular recovery. Sometimes gangrenous limbs were severed and the subject finished off with poison gas tests.

4. Poison gas use and defense. Beyond the airfield was a poison gas laboratory. It contained two chambers, one of which was used to generate gases like cyanide, phosgen, mustard gas, lewisite, or carbon monoxide. These were

piped at varying concentrations into a smaller chamber about the size of a telephone booth where the 'log' was placed. It was enclosed by glass and the effects of the gas were filmed. The poison gas team was detached to Unit 731 from the chemical warfare unit, whose headquarters were in Tsitsihar.

5. Physiology and pathology. Experiments mentioned included: exposure of the brain to test reactions to impulses; vivisection of female reproductive organs; measurement of the effect of desiccation, starvation, thirst, and lowered air pressure to the point where bowels would be extruded through the anus; transfusion of incompatible blood types; and introduction of air into arteries.

Most of the 'logs' were resistance elements, including Chinese, Korean, and some Mongol guerrillas, as well as some local Russians and Soviet military personnel captured in the course of cross-border reconnaissance or other maneuvers in the continuing tense confrontation. There is no definite evidence that prisoners from the Western allies were involved, though such cases occurred separately in Japan itself with airmen who had been shot down and captured. The victims in Pingfang put up some resistance, individuals sometimes seizing keys and attempting to escape, while on three occasions in the unit's history there were riots. Escape, however, was out of the question as the compound was surrounded by electrical barbed wire, a wall, and a trench, while the various destructive means available to the unit quickly eliminated or subdued rioters.

There are scattered reports of branch stations of this unit in Nanking, Malaysia, and elsewhere, as well as numerous episodes of the use of gas and biological warfare, mainly in China. The effect of biological warfare in China may have had certain limitations there as many of the diseases tested had been endemic, and the population would have developed greater immunity than would occur in Western countries. Ishii apparently hoped that the use of biological warfare against the latter might turn the tide in Japan's favor, but the high command seems to have heeded President Roosevelt's warning in June 1942, made with reference to poison gas, that 'retaliation in kind and full measure will be meted out.'

Immediately after the Soviet Union entered the war, Ishii and most of the unit were given top priority for evacuation to Japan after gassing the remaining 'logs' and as far as possible destroying all traces of their installations and operations. In disbanding the unit in Japan, Ishii issued three final instructions: first, that all were to conceal their military record; second, all public employment was to be avoided, as this would entail disclosure of personal histories; and third, there was to be no contact between members.

For many years, most kept these instructions, some to the grave. But among others, the network of silence gradually frayed, sometimes through the indefatigable efforts of the researchers mentioned. Sometimes it was part of a more general phenomenon, growing marked as the 1980s progressed, among aging ex-servicemen who, near the end of their lives, developed an urge to confess painful secrets before dying or at least to place their experiences into a broader life context. Among the numerous accounts of gas and biological warfare that have surfaced, Unit 731 of Harbin has remained central in this field in public consciousness, being so thoroughly documented that there has been no scope for debate of that kind that persists, for instance, about aspects of the Nanking massacre. It has been a painful issue in the field of school texts, not so much because of factual dispute but as a question of the suitability of exposing children to such horrors. This will be studied later.

Reactionary trends

These revelations and controversies during 1982 seem to have made some difference in public perceptions of the war, judging by a comparison between two surveys conducted in the late 1970s and in October 1982 on respondents' discussion of war-related topics over the preceding year. Discussion of suffering due to the war, implying 'victim consciousness,' fell from 57 percent to 41 percent; on atomic bombs (perhaps influenced by current threats of nuclear war) from 47 percent to 37 percent; on wartime society as more disciplined and dedicated from 19 percent to 9 percent; on admiration for patriotism from 21 percent to 9 percent and on the courage of the armed forces from 18 percent to 9 percent. On the other hand, discussion on the cruelty of the forces increased from 15 percent to 27 percent. Another survey in the latter month found that 51 percent of respondents considered that Japan's modern wars were a 'history of aggression' against neighboring Asian countries, as opposed to 22 percent who differed; on the other hand, 49 percent believed that Japan had been driven to such policies by its poverty of resources and the struggle to survive, as opposed to 39 percent who differed. But 83 percent agreed that contrition was appropriate for discrimination and atrocities against Chinese and Koreans in modern history, although 46 percent believed that the war could be credited as having hastened independence of Asian countries from Western oppression, while 25 percent differed from this view.

This trend away from right wing or nationalistic perceptions was, however, to undergo some degree of reversal under the prime ministership of Nakasone Yasuhiro, which began in the following month. As mentioned, he was a member of the Dietmen's 'Old Navy Club' and his rise to prominence had been watched with misgivings in some quarters as to the reactionary trends he was likely to promote. His accession marked another break in the succession of 'Yoshida school' ex-bureaucrats, like that of Tanaka earlier, and it was owing to the support of the still powerful and well-financed Tanaka faction that he was able to become prime minister. He retained the position until late 1987, a longer term than was usual under the customary rotation among the mainstream bureaucratic factions. During this time, he became notorious for adopting a more 'presidential style' in centralizing information and decision-making than has been usual in Japan in any period. He described his perception of his task on these lines:

> A large number of Japanese today have a feeling that the nation is plunging more deeply into a period of crisis and confusion such has never been experienced before.... There is worry as to what is going to happen to Japan, an uneasy sense that perhaps the nation has already reached an impasse, that growth may be over and decline imminent. (Large 1992).

As a solution, he proposed 'settling the accounts of postwar politics,' meaning the abandonment of the 'Yoshida doctrine' of economism and the minimum of purely defensive armament, replacing it with the translation of Japanese economic power into political initiative on the international scene. For this purpose he advocated constitutional revision to abolish Article 9 because 'true independence is impossible so long as a nation chooses to depend in large measure on the military power of another country for its territorial security.' He hoped to obtain leverage from the 'new Cold War' between the Soviet Union and the Western bloc arising from the invasion of Afghanistan. This incident did not involve China as in the earlier phases of the Cold War, as China had long been on very bad terms with the Soviet Union. The joint statement with Japan on the occasion of normalization in 1972 had included 'opposition to attempts by any country or group of countries to establish hegemony in the Asia-Pacific region,' an habitual code for the Soviet bloc.

At the beginning of 1983, even before his first Diet policy speech, Nakasone visited South Korea, where he promised economic aid to the extent of $4 billion and together with the president issued a joint statement affirming close cooperation, as well as commending South Korea's defense effort. He then visited the United States for talks with President Reagan, also well known for a hawkish inclination, and began a close relationship with him. They were described as being on first name terms as 'Ron and Yasu,' and Japan and the United States agreed to constitute a 'community of destiny spanning the Pacific Ocean,' with special reference to military cooperation.

In an interview with the *Washington Post,* Nakasone described Japan's role, borrowing a wartime phrase of Winston Churchill's, as an 'unsinkable aircraft carrier' and a powerful bulwark against any Soviet long distance bombing offensive. The four straits within and adjoining Japan could be used to block Soviet naval operations into the Pacific—the same sort of logic that, at the beginning of the century, had persuaded Britain to conclude the Anglo-Japanese Alliance to contain imperial Russian expansionism, with Korea as Japan's reward. Japan was also described as sharing responsibility for securing international sea lanes in its region. Subsequently, although there was a long-standing ban on arms export by Japan, an exchange of military technology was initiated and the Self Defense Agency announced that U.S. warships

55

carrying nuclear weapons could be escorted by Japanese Self Defense craft, as well as being in practice, if not quite explicitly, allowed to call at Japanese ports.

On Nakasone's return to Japan he delivered his Diet policy speech on these lines:

> I am keenly aware that Japan stands at a major turning point in its postwar history. This is the time for us to make a serious study, from prewar and postwar history, as to what to retain for later generations, what to revise and in what direction we are to proceed, using it as a pointer to a new advance.... Even in regard to institutions and systems hitherto fundamental, we must review them frankly with a new vision, without observing any taboo. (Rekishi Kyoikusha Kyogikai, 1995)

In the following month, however, he felt it was necessary to calm Chinese fears about his intentions and not only referred to the war against China in a Diet speech as a 'war of aggression' but sent the Secretary-General of the LDP on a visit to China to reassure the Chinese that no danger was presented by 'remnant militarist forces' in Japan. Precipitate action was inhibited both by international pressures and by factional complexities at home and Nakasone realized that reeducation on both public and school levels was the only means to achieve a long-term change in the postwar Japanese outlook.

He had previously been involved in establishing a Provisional Education Research Committee under cabinet control which now recommended the establishment of a Provisional Education Council directly under the cabinet and independent of the Education Ministry, with the aim of undertaking a fundamental revision of postwar school education. The Council was established in 1984 and consisted largely of Nakasone's 'brain trust' and representatives of the financial world. Its head, directly appointed by the Prime Minister, had participated in the National Congress to Establish an Autonomous Constitution (i.e., as distinct from the U.S. imposed one), while one of his deputies, a banker, was a member of what was called in Orwellian style the Peace Problems Research Committee, a personal advisory body to Nakasone studying issues of military expenditure. Nakasone had hoped to break the traditional limitation on defense expenditure to within 1 percent of GNP and, although opposition prevented this on the previous basis, it was achieved in practice by a change in accounting procedure. One member of the Council's management committee had served in the Army General Staff and was now an advisor to a top ranking trading company.

The Council submitted four reports up to April 1987, making such recommendations as greater diversity in educational institutions, tighter control over teachers and textbooks, and compulsory use of the flag and national anthem. Its activities led to a major change in educational policy which will be described later though, in a rapidly changing context, the results ultimately fell far short of Nakasone's hopes.

In September 1984, in the course of his cultivation of close relations with South Korea in the 'new Cold War' framework, Nakasone made a major gesture calculated to counter the lingering intense resentment of Japan's colonial record in Korea—perhaps only paralleled in the world of postcolonial relations by Irish bitterness at Britain's record. He invited President Chun Doohwan to make a state visit and at a reception in the palace had the Emperor utter something of an apology for Japan's colonialism along the lines: 'I truly regret the unhappy past that existed between our two countries at a certain period during this century.' Although such moves improved relations for a time at the official level, the gulf in South Korea between the military dictatorship and the mass of the people, particularly after the massacre of pro-democracy demonstrators at Kwangju in 1980, meant that the popular mind was far from impressed. This became clear under Chun's successor, Roh Tae-wu, when formal claims came to be raised against Japan, beginning with those by the large numbers of wartime conscript laborers.

From mid-1985, Nakasone launched a psychological offensive to promote his agenda for neonationalist revival. At an LDP seminar in July, he denounced both the 'Tokyo trial' view and the Marxist view of history, if held by Japanese, as 'masochistic,' which became a favorite description among right wing revisionists. He showed a preference for 'Greater East Asia War' and urged constitutional revision in the words:

> Self defense is the most basic factor in safeguarding the country and the lives and property of the nation. If the state suffers aggression there will be no constitution or anything else. It is therefore proper that, when a constitution exists, measures be taken adequate to ensure its existence. (Rekishi Kyoikusha Kyogikai 1995)

He emphasized the Emperor's role, describing Japan in prewar terms as a 'family state centered on the Emperor.' He also raised the question of an official visit to the Yasukuni shrine to the war dead on the next War Dead Commemoration Day the following month. He and other cabinet ministers, like the Emperor himself, had always been in the habit of visiting it in a private capacity, but now he wished to make it official as a symbolic rehabilitation of patriotic sentiment. He hoped that it might also lead to the passage of a bill for state support for the shrine, which had been repeatedly blocked by more moderate factions who invoked the constitutional ban on government support for any religious activities. He noted that the proposed visit was being actively discussed in the party and that cabinet had set up a study group to explore the constitutional implications. He promised that he would give calm consideration to its report and reach a decision in the light of national opinion, the attitude of all political parties and the views of the majority of LDP members.

An official visit was made, but this brought a hostile reaction from China, both Koreas, and Southeast Asia almost comparable to the earlier textbook uproar. As the names of Tojo and other military figures executed as war criminals had meanwhile been entered on the shrine's list of spirits, an official visit was construed as legitimizing the war that they had launched.

As foreign denunciations were reinforced by domestic condemnation as well, Nakasone attempted to moderate his position by stating that he appreciated his critics' viewpoint, but this in turn provoked a massive right wing rally to press for state support for the shrine, attended also by members of the LDP's own right wing. As the resulting situation was clearly too explosive, the essentially pragmatic mainstream of the party ensured that the provocation was not repeated in the following year, when Nakasone refrained from visiting the shrine at all. On the eve of War Dead Commemoration Day, the cabinet Chief Secretary announced that there would be no official visit because that of the previous year had 'given rise to criticism among neighboring countries, which had undergone great suffering and loss throughout the country's past actions, to the effect that it amounted to worship of class A war criminals responsible for those actions.'

A few days later, to a question in the Diet by a Communist party member, the Chief Secretary replied that the government accepted the verdict of the Tokyo Trials in accordance with the San Francisco peace treaty. Early the next month, Nakasone himself in a conference of media chiefs stated that he considered the war to be an aggressive war. Not long afterwards, this stance was put to a test when the Education Minister, Fujio Masayuki, in an article in *Bungei Shunju,* cast doubt on the received account of the Nanking massacre and suggested that, although Japan's annexation of Korea was described as aggression, there were historical justifications for it. The Chinese government demanded his dismissal and Nakasone complied, going still further to placate South Korea by a personal visit.

As a *Mainichi* political analyst expressed it, he had been forced to weigh the contrasting goals of promoting national identity and developing Japan's international role and had decided in favor of the latter. Another factor was the new phase of *detente* between the United States and the Soviet Union initiated in the Geneva conference of the previous year, which reduced leverage for change based on defense needs. So when Nakasone came to step down in 1987, with the return to power of 'Yoshida school' type bureaucrats, it was clear that nothing so fundamental as constitutional revision was yet feasible. The combination of left wing and pacifistic resistance with the pragmatism of most LDP factions and their financial backers turned out to be, as in the past, a remarkably strong barrier to any radical change, especially when reinforced by criticism from abroad, to which most Japanese opinion has been sensitive. At the same time, however, the mood created in some quarters by Nakasone's rhetoric had provided a new stimulus to right wing revisionism, which subsequently became increasingly evident. Fujio's indiscreet remarks turned out to be only the first of a series of such provocations by prominent political figures in succeeding years.

War literature and education: The Okinawa campaign

Earlier in 1986 another international protest had been raised, this time again in the field of education, over the preparation and authorization of a much more nationalistic textbook than any hitherto, called *A New History of Japan,* designed for senior high school. It had been compiled mainly by the National Congress to Safeguard Japan, a lobby organization aimed at wholesale constitutional revision. Affiliated to it were such bodies as the Japan Teachers' Association, an organization opposing the mainstream and left wing Japan Teachers' Union; the House of Longevity, a syncretistic religious-philosophical movement; and the Association of Shinto shrines. It published a periodical called *Breath of Japan* and had undertaken to produce the textbook as part of the celebrations for the 60th anniversary of the Emperor's accession—something that the Nakasone cabinet was also promoting.

The book was frankly described as aiming at the 'formation of an ideological trend towards constitutional revision.' More details, given in a press conference, were that the text had:

> Developed a cultural direction for comprehending the special features of traditional Japanese culture by relating it to political, economic, and social trends in each period; employed honorific language for the Emperor, recognizing the indispensable character of the Emperor in history; in ancient history it had not been constrained by archeological remains and references in foreign histories [Chinese and Korean] but respected Japanese histories such as the earliest chronicles, for example clarifying ancient thought through their myths.

The chronicles referred to form Japan's earliest historical literature, compiled in its present form in the Eighth Century A.D., which, although containing considerable historical data, also included foundation myths, usually avoided in postwar education because of their close association with prewar nationalistic ideology. The textbook, however, was so slanted in that direction that it should have been disqualified under the Basic Education Law which, as mentioned earlier, prescribed political neutrality in education. But this provision was essentially aimed against left wing bias and in this case was not applied against its right wing counterpart. Postwar historiography had aimed at more objective treatment by emphasizing alternatives to the native tradition such as Chinese or Korean sources or archeological remains in Japan itself, the proper evaluation of which had earlier been inhibited by State Shinto

59

dogma. The *New History* sought to reemphasize native tradition, though of course without quite the literalism of prewar education.

Other factors that would normally have led to its disqualification were numerous factual slips and production flaws, partly due to the haste with which it had been prepared to meet the imperial anniversary. But the screening process did not fully consider these, counting only a proportion small enough to avoid disqualification. The book's general contents were, however, reported through the media before the procedure was completed and aroused protests from Asian countries for its justification of Japanese expansionism from the 19th century on. The Foreign Ministry therefore pressed the authors to moderate their treatment, which they did, with much resistance, to the minimum extent needed to pass screening. This was finally ensured by pressure from Nakasone himself, who described the book as 'a good text which must definitely be authorized.' But he also personally visited Beijing to reassure the Chinese government that their views were being respected and unduly controversial material avoided.

When the sample copy became available, it was found to have many more faults than the Textbook Screening Council had acknowledged. Cases were found on historical maps where the traditional swastika symbol for a Buddhist temple had been reversed, doubtless inadvertently, to the Nazi type. North Sakhalin was described as annexed after the Russo-Japanese War, though only the south had been; in a map of the age of exploration, the Straits of Magellan were filled in as land; scales were wrong. The sample was therefore quite exceptionally provided with an errata table. In the event, it was only selected by a very few schools, most or all being prefectural schools in Fukuoka in Kyushu, a historic center of nationalism and Pan-Asianism. At the beginning of the century it had been the place of origin of a well-known expansionist society called the Amur River Society, the name indicating its aim of blocking Russian expansion beyond the Amur River into Manchuria and Korea. It played a considerable part in achieving this and opening these areas to Japanese expansion. During the lead-up to the Pacific War, it became rather celebrated under the misleading name of 'Black Dragon Society' due to a literal rendering of the Chinese name for the Amur River, the 'Black Dragon River' (Heilung-chiang). It was mistakenly blamed by the allies for the terrorism of the 1930s. It had actually always worked only with ultranationalistic elements within the establishment, though its organizational pattern did inspire some more radical right wing groups. This local tradition probably accounts for the *New History*'s adoption in that area, but its success was very limited and the publisher ceased producing it in 1993 as uneconomic, though a revised edition was then taken up by another publisher, as to be described below.

Another major textbook protest, though in this case from within Japan, had occurred when Takashima Nobuyoshi, a supporter of Ienaga, tried to include in a senior high school text for use from 1983 an authentic account of the battle of Okinawa, based on the prefectural histories of 1970. The Screening

Council deleted it on the grounds that oral history was unreliable and that only official records should be used—which of course are biased toward an official line. But 'island-wide' and 'prefecture-wide' protests from Okinawa were so vehement that the Ministry allowed such accounts to pass the next round of screening a few years later, so that the facts of this phase of the war became better known. In 1987, too, Fujiwara Akira published two volumes of studies on the battle.

U.S. forces landed on Okinawa at the beginning of April 1945, starting one of the most intense battles of the whole of the Second World War, particularly noted for the frequent use of Kamikaze suicide air attacks and human torpedoes. Fighting continued in both Okinawa and neighboring islands until 22 June, when the top commander and his staff, together with the civil governor, took their own lives. The nature of the campaign is ably summarized by Ienaga:

> Adult men and women were called up, formed into Patriotic Defense Units, and used in combat. High school students were also drafted. Some male students were armed and sent into combat; others were assigned to dig trenches, build field fortifications and serve as messengers. Female students were pressed into service as nurses to care for the wounded.
>
> The military garrison and civilians were driven to the southern tip of the island into a defensive perimeter within the Yaezu-Dake escarpment near the villages of Kiyan, Makabe and Mabuni and the caves in the seaside cliffs. Naval guns pounded the area from the ocean side. Soldiers moved closer from the land side, their flame-throwers incinerating everything in their path. Bombers blasted the defenders from the air. Food and water ran out. The wounded and sick formed a chorus of pain. Covered with blood from the wounded and dying, the girl students stayed with their patients to the end. Many civilians wanted to surrender but were prevented by the army, they committed suicide with hand grenades or bayonets. (Ienaga 1978)

As Fujiwara puts it, the garrison did not fight to protect the prefecture's inhabitants but sacrificed them to gain time for the forces in the main islands to prepare for the 'decisive battle for the homeland,' designed to secure a final stalemate and a compromise peace. This strategy was symbolized by the construction of a vast underground bunker at Matsushiro in the central mountainous region near Mt Fuji to accommodate the imperial household, the central organs of government and the supreme command. When Prince Konoe had urged the Emperor in February to work for an early peace to forestall revolution, the Emperor had instead clung to the hope that the forces might yet reverse the allies' advance to the extent needed at least to preserve the 'unique

61

national polity' centered on the Imperial House, entrusted to him by his ancestors. Okinawa was sacrificed for this.

The Self Defense Forces' version of the battle idealizes the islanders' role in such terms as: 'Earnestly praying for the fatherland's victory, they in all tranquillity collectively dispatched themselves' when resistance was no longer possible and surrender the only alternative, as the islands' limited area left no room for retreat or flight. Similarly, although independent research has clearly established the death rate of the islands' inhabitants as over 150,000 of the then prefectural total of about 600,000, the Okinawa Prefecture Relief Section of the Welfare Ministry officially puts it at 94,000, which happens to be the same as the more accurately recorded figure for armed forces deaths. In the same vein, the Self Defense Forces' account records about 10,000 cases of 'provision of shelters' by civilians for the use of the armed forces, implying that they voluntarily exposed themselves to enemy bombardment so that the army could continue resistance from the relative safety of the surrendered dugouts and caves. This concealed the reality that the forces had often expelled them from their shelters, though the fiction was in part well-intentioned as qualifying such 'volunteers' or family survivors for relief aid. The same situation applied in the case of the surrender of food stocks to the forces, as refusal meant death.

Certain sections of the population were also victims of preemptive execution on the grounds that they were unreliable and real or potential 'spies' for the enemy. They included people associated with organized labor and therefore suspected of subversion, returned immigrants from Hawaii, the Americas, or the Philippines (who had been rather numerous because of Ryukyu's limited resources), and Christian activists. Other potential 'spies' were any of the numerous inhabitants who had worked on military installations and if captured might be used as guides or informants by the enemy. So a general policy was adopted of urging suicide rather than capture, which had been common among the armed forces and was now extended to the general population. Capture was represented as the supreme shame and death for the Emperor as the supreme virtue. Women in particular were urged to die rather than face rape. But perhaps more effective than such reasoning was the sheer terror of the unknown represented by capture into alien hands.

Hand grenades were often distributed as an efficient means to this end. Some might be used against the enemy, if possible, but the last was to be saved for suicide. When such measures failed, the forces would 'assist in suicide.' Handicapped people are mentioned as being eliminated because they were of no use and a possible liability. Others killed were cases who had been captured by the Americans and released to carry messages urging surrender. Fujiwara notes that, although about 20,000 of the regular garrison troops were natives of Ryukyu, their conditioning had been such that their behavior was no different from troops from elsewhere in Japan. Another complex psychological factor was an awareness of the contempt in which other Japanese held them, which paradoxically drove them to demonstrate that their loyalty was not inferior to others—something also known among blacks, second generation Japanese, and Hispanics in the American forces. The great majority of these troops would have died and form a part of total deaths among the Ryukyu population.

Apart from direct influence from the troops, other types of deaths included children, even killed by their parents to prevent their crying from betraying a hiding place. Fathers or elder brothers sometimes killed their own families to save them from a 'worse fate.' A survivor from Tokashiki Island, where the Americans had landed a little earlier than Okinawa, recalls that when hand grenades ran out or failed to explode, 'husbands killed wives, parents killed children, brothers killed sisters, either strangling them with cords, striking their heads with clubs or stones, cutting their throats with sickles or razors or any other method they could think of.' Two Korean comfort women attached to the island's garrison survived, one of whom, Pae Pong-gi, later continued in prostitution with the Americans on Okinawa and in 1979 became the first publicly known comfort woman through figuring in a film called *An Old Lady in Okinawa: Testimony of a Military Comfort Woman*.

The Thai-Burma Railway

During the mid-1980s, some public attention was also drawn to another notorious episode of the war—the Thai-Burma Railway. In 1979, the Yasukuni Shrine had been presented with a locomotive from that railway by survivors of its wartime construction unit, who had raised funds to buy it from the Thai government. To them this was merely a memento of their dedication in that most arduous project—the 'death railway' that had cost the lives of so many allied prisoners and many more Asian laborers. But other former members of the unit, organized by a former Kempeitai interpreter using the pseudonym Nagase, had a little earlier adopted a different mode of commemoration by way of arranging help for surviving laborers who had settled in areas along the line, having been unable to return home amid postwar disorder. Nagase also arranged a reunion with some former prisoners of war at a bridge on the River Kwai, already well known in Japan from a film of that name. A British former prisoner there gave him a book he had written, describing his wartime experiences under the title *And the Dawn came up like Thunder*. Nagase at his own expense published a translation of it in Japan in 1980 entitled *Slaves on the Thai-Burma Railway*. It made little initial impact because of limited distribution but in 1983 inspired a party of teachers belonging to the Geography Teachers Research Association to visit wartime sites in Southeast Asia to expand awareness of the area. In 1984 they arranged for a reissue of the book with added material by a regular publisher mainly for use as general reading by students, with considerable success. In 1986 also a leading publisher brought out *Fiction and Fact in 'Bridge on the River Kwai'* based on immediate postwar investigations on the railway in conjunction with the British army. One fictional point was that the bridge was not actually destroyed as in the film. In the same year, a Buddhist Peace Temple was dedicated beside another bridge on the railway by joint local and Japanese initiative, with coverage in Japan.

Singapore

In 1985 and 1986, four books were published dealing in detail with the wartime massacres of overseas Chinese in Singapore and other aspects of Japanese occupation there. Although in most occupied areas the Japanese set up or retained local administrative entities which were supposedly destined to become voluntary partners in the co-prosperity sphere, Singapore was treated as a direct colony, partly because of its strategic importance and partly because it had been the major center of anti-Japanese agitation by Chinese in Southeast Asia, as well as financial support for resistance in China itself.

It was renamed Shonan (Syonan in the then romanization), meaning 'Brilliant South,' the character *sho* for 'brilliant' being derived from the Emperor's reign title of Showa or 'Brilliant Harmony.' Immediately after the fall of Singapore in February 1942, the Japanese rounded up about 200,000 of the male Chinese population for a 'general inquisition' and executed all who had volunteered for defense units or were regarded as having been anti-Japanese activists—a large proportion of the whole. This massacre was remembered in Singapore as the *sook-ching,* a Chinese form of the Japanese term for a political purge. It was the beginning of four years of intense suppression, both ideological and economic.

In 1967, the Singapore government and the Chinese Chamber of Commerce erected a monument 68 meters high in the War Memorial Park over the collected remains of the victims. About ten years afterwards, a Japanese businessman visiting Singapore came across this monument and wishing to photograph it, without at first realizing its significance, asked a young Chinese couple nearby to pose for him to give the scale. At this, the male of the pair grew furious, and it was only then that the visitor examined the inscription. In Chinese characters clearly intelligible to a Japanese it read: 'Memorial to the Holocaust of Citizens under the Japanese Occupation.' So, in the hope that future Japanese might be better educated on such matters and avoid giving offense as he had, he undertook thorough research into the fall of Singapore and in 1985 published *In the Wake of Murder: The Massacre of the Singapore Chinese.* In the same year, another book on the subject was published by Ms Matsui Yayori of the *Asahi* who later became well known in connection with the comfort women issue. She interviewed the second former comfort woman to become publicly known, a Korean who had remained in Thailand after the war and married there, being best known by the Thai name of Yuyuta. Two more books on wartime Singapore appeared in the following year.

Broad compilations

Publications covering wider fields of the war continued to appear during the decade. One type, quite numerous but not widely circulated, consisted of unit histories, compiled by 'Comrades Associations.' These were usually not offered for sale but produced only for the interest of unit members and their families. Large numbers, however, are held in the National Diet Library, and a study made of these indicated that their output reached a peak in the early 1980s. They are described as generally governed by the officers' perspective, with little expression of the common troops' feelings or attitudes. Naturally, in view of their intended readership, they avoided issues like aggression or atrocities. The author of a 1985 publication *Luzon War Chronicle* on the Philippines criticized the procedure of comrades associations' memorial services and publications in these terms:

> In these cases, the demand is strong that for the sake of the fallen heroes and bereaved families, the misery of battle and aspects shameful to the forces should not be described. For their sake, it is attempted to conceal the tragic and ugly side of battle. Only aspects favorable to the former forces are described, ignoring dark and brutal facts. (Yoshida 1995)

Much more authentic and widely circulated was a major effort undertaken by the *Asahi* over 1986-87. It called for contributions to a 'War' series under its 'Theme Parlor' column. About 4,200 pieces were received, of which 1,145 were published, causing the series to run far longer than expected, for 13 months. In 1987, the published pieces were collected in book form in two volumes under the title *The War,* which became a best-seller. Most pieces consisted of personal reminiscences of experience in the forces and, in contrast with the constraints of unit histories, many of them refused to shrink from admission of aggression, infliction of harm, and atrocities. Contributors included former members of Unit 731, who had earlier collaborated in *The Devil's Gluttony,* and others who could testify firsthand about the Nanking massacre. Many were also eloquent about the wretched conditions of the lower ranks of the Japanese troops themselves. One had kept count of the number of times he was beaten as a young conscript in the normal course of what is described in English as 'bastardization,' his total coming to 264.

Even in postwar captivity in Siberia the treatment of lower ranks by their officers did not improve.

Told to punish a soldier who had stolen pig food, the commanding officer and other officers took him to the bath and stripped him. Putting lumps of snow into a tub of cold water, they rubbed the man's body with the slush and placed him in a cell. The temperature was -30 degrees centigrade. He died a few days later. His best friend is still not able to tell the details of his death to the family.

Apart from the experience in the forces, many pieces dealt with air raids, evacuation from the city, labor mobilization, and repatriation, especially from Manchuria. The prevailing mood expressed was an urge to place the tragedies of war on record. As an afterword to the publication says, 'The special feature of this series to be noted is that the side of the injuring party emerges strongly in the form of remorse for injuries committed, the killing of inhabitants of enemy territories or even one's own compatriots, or having to abandon them.' (Fujiwara 1988)

Still another class of contributor belonged to a younger generation emphatically raising charges of war responsibility against their elders. But the series as a whole is described as 'pulsating with contempt and hatred for the ruling elite who directed the war and their henchmen, together with the social and political system they imposed.'

Naval studies: Court and Emperor

At another level, the vogue of naval studies, related to 'strategic' or 'naval style' management, continued and reached its peak during this decade, though with changes of emphasis. A corollary of this current on the contemporary social scene was the observation that men who had held high rank in the navy had also been comparably successful in civil life, notably those with background in the 'short term active service navy paymaster' category to which Nakasone himself belonged. Their situation was contrasted with that of ex-army men whose later success rate bore little relation to their army rank. The two prime ministers of army background, Tanaka and Suzuki, had only been privates. This meant that, in such an obsessively status-conscious society as Japan (though not class-obsessed in the British sense), it was more difficult for groups with army backgrounds to develop effectively because of changes or ambiguities in status, whereas ex-navy groups, with an even greater rank consciousness, had preserved more consistency of status in their careers and therefore more group continuity. Several studies were published on this theme with titles such as *The Unending Navy* (1978), *The Navy: Political and Financial Leaders and their Secret Sentiments* (1985), *Figures with an Enduring Future* (1985) and *Study of the Short Term Active Service Paymasters* (1987).

Since Nakasone as prime minister symbolized this perception at a national level, it was natural that under his ascendancy the cult of navy style management should attract continuing attention, with a corollary in a vogue of naval wartime studies evolving into a distinctive 'naval view of history.' This, as in the earliest postwar literature, tended again to focus on the Pacific phase of the war as against its Asian aspects. Organizational type studies, however, now tended towards more searchingly critical investigations of the reasons for wartime failures under such titles as *The Essence of Failure* (1984), *The Combined Fleets Fiasco* (1987), and the three volume *Zero Fighters Burning* (1984-1990). This changed approach as contrasted with earlier optimism is seen as reflecting growing problems in Japanese management and economy, and the intent of these studies is often described in terms of their being 'case studies on teaching material for contemporary management courses.' Naval style management was no longer seen as a guarantee of success but a subject for problematic analysis.

The more purely historical naval studies of the time, however, took a more positive view at least of the historical figures they centered on. From 1982 to 1986 appeared four volumes of biographical studies of Admiral Inoue Shigeyoshi, portrayed with some reason as liberal and antiwar. In the early 1930s, he had been a member of the navy's 'treaty faction' who supported acceptance of the limitations set by the London Naval Treaty of 1930, as against the 'Fleet faction' in the Naval General Staff. These regarded the treaty as treasonable in that the cabinet had ignored the constitutionally independent General Staff, relying exclusively on the navy Ministry in the treaty negotiations. Admiral Inoue was also on record as opposing the Axis alliance and war with the United States. On the tactical side, he had opposed the current big battleship doctrine, which gave Japan the largest warships in the world, and foresaw the dominant role that was to be played by the air arm.

A two volume study of Admiral Yonai Mitsumasa, published in 1990, followed similar lines, also with some justification. As Navy Minister in 1939, he, together with the Foreign Minister, blocked the then cabinet's plans for a military alliance with the Axis until the Hitler-Stalin pact undermined such plans for a time. Subsequently, as prime minister he maintained his stand until his cabinet fell through the army's withdrawal of his War Minister when Axis victories in Europe made the alliance seem an irresistible opportunity. The armed forces, to cope with the crisis following the 1936 coup attempt, had regained their earlier prerogative of nominating their cabinet ministers from the active service list, a privilege that the army thenceforward used to dominate cabinet formation and dismissal.

A critic, however, notes certain flaws in the treatment of these figures. Inoue, though a moderate in relations with the United States, was an advocate of ruthless bombing of China, while Yonai, in being questioned in 1946 by war crimes investigators, stated that he considered Hitler's essential fault lay in rashly attempting to accomplish epoch-making objectives in an unrealistically short time frame, rather than necessarily being at fault in his aims themselves. Nevertheless, the literature of this period tended to confirm and perpetuate the widespread view of the navy as a whole as having been more liberal, rational, and moderate than the army and so tending to absolve it of a major share of responsibility for the war. This, of course, does betray a sense that the war itself was unjustifiable, so undermining the right wing revisionist 'affirmation of the Greater East Asia War.'

The same may be said of a parallel 'Court Group view of History' which was emerging in this period when the Emperor was clearly dying and a need was felt to evaluate his reign in its overall perspective. The group referred to consisted of the Emperor's closest advisors such as elder statesmen, former prime ministers, the Lord Privy Seal, the Grand Chamberlain, and the Imperial Household Minister, together with their intimates. They tend to be treated as 'aristocratic conservative liberals' who retained the values of early 20th century liberalism and pro-British leanings and resisted the military's drive to political domination and war.

This view of course ultimately stemmed from the 'bargain' between occupation and establishment to exempt the Emperor from any involvement in war trials, which were in turn designed to narrow the range of war responsibility along the lines noted earlier. It began to take a more systematic shape in some of the studies of the 1970s based on the diaries of wartime officials then available. In the 1980s it took a more coherent form under such titles as the two volume *Showa History of Senior Statesmen* (1981), *Prime Minister Suzuki Kantaro* [the last wartime prime minister] (1982), *Showa History of Emperor Hirohito* [using his normally taboo name to humanize him] and *Emperor Hirohito's Five Decisions* (both 1984), together with *The Sacred Decision* [to end the war] (1985).

The convergence of this historiographical stream with the naval one is strengthened by the Emperor's particular trust in such naval figures as Admiral Okada Keisuke, another member of the 'treaty faction,' who as prime minister was an assassination target in the 1936 coup attempt, and Yonai, who was also threatened with assassination for blocking the Axis alliance. This treatment of course is centered on the Emperor, portraying him, as he did himself, as a constitutional monarch who was bound to accept the advice of his ministers even if he disagreed with it. The problem here is that he was also commander-in-chief of the armed forces, whose general staffs were responsible directly to him independently of cabinet. Regarding the Court Group as a whole, who were also quite separate from the cabinet and are represented in this literature as a countervailing force to the army, closer studies on the original documents which continued to appear indicate rather a steady shift away from the liberal and pacifistic inclinations which they did indeed hold until the early 1930s.

Debate on the role of Emperor and Court was very much broadened during and after his last illness and death, which occurred at the beginning of 1989. This led immediately both to the release of new documents and a corresponding psychological release from inhibitions that had affected many mainstream

Japanese during his lifetime. His final illness occupied most of his last year and was recognized as terminal from September. As the media from then on constantly monitored his health, much of society adopted a posture of what was called 'self-restraint,' manifested in an abnormal degree of austerity in life style, becoming conspicuous in the low-key approach to the normally bustling New Year festive season. Business was so severely affected that the Crown Prince was prevailed on to call for moderation. This rather unexpected public reaction was perhaps not due to any definite sentiment regarding the Emperor so much as the deeply ingrained sense of propriety in Japanese society, especially in relation to death related rituals. Perhaps most potent was an overpowering sense of the end of a long and most eventful era that had occupied the whole lives of almost all of the then population, having just reached its 64th year. The prevailing atmosphere is described as 'muted oppressive, as though on the cusp of a storm.' (Buruma 1994)

Into this atmosphere there suddenly intruded a most discordant note. On 7 December, the anniversary of the Pearl Harbor attack, a Communist member of the Nagasaki city assembly, pursuing a familiar role among members of his party, asked the mayor, Motoshima Hitoshi, what he thought on the question of the Emperor's responsibility for the war. The mayor replied:

> Forty-three years have passed since the end of the war and I think we have had enough chance to reflect on the nature of that war. From various accounts from abroad and having been a soldier myself, involved in military education, I do believe that the Emperor bore some responsibility for the war. (Buruma 1994)

He implied in particular that the Emperor could have spared his city the horror of atomic attack by ending the war sooner. The next day the regional branch of the LDP, to which he belonged, as well as some fellow assemblymen, demanded that he retract his statement, but he refused and was dismissed as counselor to the LDP association. The disciplinary committee stated that 'it was an act of extreme indiscretion for a public official to have made a public statement like that.' Even close associates and overt sympathizers were puzzled by his bluntness under those particular circumstances and some speculated that, as he belonged to a Christian family of long standing, his background must have distanced him from the prevailing Japanese ethos. In a press conference, he persisted:

> I am not saying that the Emperor alone was responsible for the war. Many people were, myself included. But I do feel the present state of politics is abnormal. Any statement about the Emperor becomes an emotional issue. Freedom of speech should not be limited by time or place. In a democracy we respect even those whose opinions we don't share. (Buruma 1994)

A week later, right wing extremists, following a familiar pattern, drove 30 loudspeaker trucks through Nagasaki calling for Motoshima's death as 'divine retribution'—their traditional formula to incite assassination, dating from long before the war. This exercise was soon afterwards repeated by 82 trucks carrying members from 62 right wing groups from throughout Japan. The LDP prefectural governor declared his stand as one of refusal to cooperate with him as mayor. Conservative associations and the prefectural office for Shinto shrines called for his impeachment. The Mayor of Hiroshima, though as usual in that city a strong supporter of the antiwar movement, refused to support Motoshima despite the shared experience of atomic attack.

On the other hand, within two weeks 13,684 signatures supporting him were presented to the city hall by a newly formed Nagasaki Citizens Committee for Free Speech, and over the next few months he received 300,000 letters of support from people in a great variety of walks of life, including some army veterans. As in such cases, the *Asahi* letters column amply represented the debate, the majority of writers supporting him. He did attend the Emperor's funeral on 24 February, along with members of all political parties, though this did not save him from an assassination attempt in the following January, which he barely survived. But he remained in office as Mayor, sustained by his personal network and general popularity.

The Emperor in retrospect

Over the couple of years following the Emperor's death, the publication of writings by individuals who had known him rapidly 'became a torrent.' (Bix 1992) In 1990 alone, six diaries bearing on his career were published, providing considerable alternative material to that promoting the 'Court Group view.' Most sensational of all the new sources, however, was one originating from the Emperor himself, formally called 'The Showa Emperor's Eight-hour Monologue.' He had dictated this in five sessions over March to April 1946 when preparations for the war trials were proceeding and decisions on its conduct were not yet quite final. His aides had conveyed to him a series of questions from occupation GHQ seeking to clarify key issues bearing on the trials. In the company of five aides, he dictated replies along lines framed over some months of discussions with intimates.

The text later produced as the Monologue was taken down by one of the aides, Terasaki Hidenari, the Emperor's usual interpreter and go-between to GHQ, who had up to the war served in the Embassy in Washington. After his death in 1951, his half-American daughter kept his papers and finally gave this manuscript to the *Bungei Shunju,* which published it at the end of 1990. The next year it appeared in book form with Terasaki's diary and sold 140,000 copies in a few months.

The Monologue ranges over the whole period from the beginning of expansionist intrigues in army circles in 1928 up to the end of the war. Although of course not comparing in degree of detail with the voluminous diaries and memoirs left by leading court and military figures, it is regarded as presenting a revealing picture of the Emperor's attitudes. Though with ambiguities, it does not square well with the 'Court Group view' representing him as essentially aloof from and basically averse to the military's belligerent policies. He only criticizes actions by the military when these were due to lower level elements defying control by their superiors, never when they had been decided by due process under his authority. Even then, he expresses some sympathy for hot-heads reacting against the caution of politicians in the mounting crisis of the early 1930s:

> Because the military stood up under such circumstances, shouldering the frustrations of the nation, it was extremely difficult to check the spirited young men who formed its core, even though they acted recklessly without regard to means. For their reckless behavior appeared to exhibit some common ground with the patriotic action of freeing the state from deadlock. (Bix 1992)

The two causes of the war that he considered most basic were racism and oil, the first referring to long-term tensions with the West typified by Japan's failure to obtain a declaration of racial equality at the Versailles Peace Conference and color-based immigration restrictions in California and Australia; the second to the war's immediate trigger in the oil embargo imposed after the Japanese move into southern French Indochina.

Sometimes he expresses a sense of constraints on his range of options, either from the formal political process or from the danger of extralegal violence. Under the former:

> So-called imperial conferences were strange affairs. All the participants who attended them, with the exception of the president of the Privy Council, had already agreed on everything beforehand at cabinet meetings or liaison conferences [with the general staffs]. Thus only one person, the president of the Privy Council, was in a position to express a dissenting opinion on a proposal. (Bix 1992)

Regarding the latter type of problem:

> Let us assume that I had vetoed the decision to go to war. I think it would certainly have led to enormous civil strife at home.... Ultimately, a furious war would have developed anyway and would have brought about a tragedy far worse than this war. In the end [for lack of a stable source of authority] Japan would have been destroyed. (Bix 1992)

71

Occasionally, however, he does admit to initiatives at a less formal level which, in Japan particularly, can be more significant than formal processes. Some examples:

> [Regarding the limited Shanghai incident of 1932] the suspension of hostilities on March 3 did not occur by the formal issuance of an official imperial order, but by my having expressly ordered [General] Shirakawa beforehand not to expand the conflict. (Bix 1992)
>
> I wanted to strike the enemy just once, anywhere, and quickly obtain the chance for peace [by negotiation]. But having given a firm promise to Germany not to make a unilateral peace, I did not for reasons of international trust, want to discuss peace before Germany did. Therefore I even went so far as to want Germany to be defeated as quickly as possible. (Bix 1992)

In a contrasting mood:

> At the beginning when the United States and Britain planned to conquer [French] Africa, I warned Tojo to recommend to the Germans that rather than give priority to their war against the Soviet Union, they should give priority to Africa.
>
> After being defeated in Okinawa, we could not devise any plans for a naval battle. Thinking that our last ray of hope was that we might be able to inflict considerable damage on Britain and the United States if we attacked Yunnan in concert with the Burma campaign, I told this to [army chief of staff] Umezu but he disagreed, saying that we could no longer continue supplying the troops. (Bix 1992)

The initiatives the Emperor admits to here, as well as a number of additional cases appearing in other material concurrently becoming available do not seem very well-conceived or successful when adopted by the high command, so the degree of his responsibility or effectiveness in the conduct of the war, although not negligible, leaves considerable room for debate, which continues. It probably ceased to be felt as a central issue. In the month after his death, a Jiji Press Agency survey found that 45 percent of respondents regarded him as bearing some responsibility for the war and 8 percent full responsibility, while only 29 percent denied any responsibility; yet 66 percent expressed respect for him, so that a sizable proportion did not regard this as incompatible with some degree of war responsibility. This must relate to the widespread problem of the diffusion of responsibility often noted in Japanese organizations.

In any case, the counterattack against the 'Court Group view' was pursued energetically over the next few years under such titles as *The Showa Em-*

peror's Direction of the War (1990), the eight volume *Documentation on the Showa Emperor* (1984-1993), *The Showa Emperor's Fifteen Year War* (1991 by Fujiwara Akira), *The Showa Emperor as Supreme Commander* (1994), and *Politics and Society in the Fifteen Year War Period* (1995).

5 The nineties

In the early 1990s, public consciousness of the Asia-Pacific War received a new stimulus from a series of group lawsuits against Japan demanding individual compensation for injuries suffered due to the war. Up to this time, Japan had assumed, without challenge from elsewhere, that such claims had been appropriately settled at the national level under the San Francisco peace treaty and the other agreements mentioned. But as the Cold War subsided, along with accompanying inhibitions in other countries—Communist or non-Communist, Asian or Western—numerous individuals affected by the war began to consider litigation against Japan. This was largely because Japanese payments under reparations or economic aid had rarely provided relief to actual victims of the war, although this purported to be part of the aim of such funds.

An early move towards prospective litigation was the formation in 1972, in Japan and South Korea, of Korean Forced Draft Investigation Groups to gather data on the large number of Koreans drafted for labor in Japan, totaling about 990,000. They had been paid at rates well below that of equivalent Japanese laborers and were often owed severance pay, forming a large part of the earnings due to them, which had been cut off by the end of the war and their repatriation. Many had also died from grueling working and living conditions. In 1979, some of these laborers who had been stranded in Southern Sakhalin when that colony was overrun by Soviet forces began litigation for compensation from Japan, though this was suspended for a time in 1989 when improved relations between the Soviet Union (soon to be dissolved) and South Korea made their repatriation to the South possible. Meanwhile, however, a precedent for individual compensation was set in 1987 when Japan agreed to pay $20,000 each to Taiwanese incapacitated from service in the Japanese forces and to bereaved families of those killed.

The labor draft issue began to take a definite direction in May 1990 when President Roh Tae-wu of South Korea made a state visit to Japan. On that occasion the new Emperor much improved on his father's earlier expression of regret to President Chun with the words: 'I cannot contain my sense of remorse in recalling the suffering undergone by your people in that unhappy period precipitated by my country.' This, however, still did not satisfy the Korean public, some of whom felt the words to be bizarre or forced. A survey found that only 8 percent were satisfied with the statement as an apology, while 79 percent were dissatisfied. Rather interestingly, dissatisfaction was highest in the twenties age group, who were furthest from having experienced Japanese rule. As this generation, however, had also long been bitterly hostile to their own military-dominated regime, to the extent of frequent bloody rioting and even insurrection, it seems that resentment of Japan may have fused with that of their own government, in view of the latter's reliance on Japanese aid. Prime Minister Kaifu apologized in more direct terms, as he also did a year later on a visit to the ASEAN countries, where in a speech in Singapore he spoke of 'sternly reflecting on my country's actions which brought unbearable suffering and sorrow to many in the Asia-Pacific region.'

During President's Roh's visit, the Korean representatives requested help from the Japanese government to obtain data on the labor draft and a good deal was provided, though gaps remained either through the loss of records or perhaps concealment. But the Japanese acceded to another request for relief to Korean victims of atomic bomb attacks who had returned to Korea and were not reached by measures available to those remaining in Japan. A foundation was formed to assist them, with funds to amount to ¥4 billion over some years. This provided another type of precedent in relation to later litigation.

Investigations on the labor draft soon extended to a related issue that proved more emotional and commanded widespread attention both domestically and internationally—the exposure of the wartime comfort women system. To readers of war literature it came as no surprise, as comfort women (the official term used in the forces though not in public use during the war) were often mentioned and some writers had published studies on them. Besides, it was fairly well known among readers of general history that camp followers and military brothels were a common accompaniment of wars everywhere, and they were still conspicuous around U.S. bases in Japan and Korea. So the theme had never been politicized, particularly as no surviving comfort women had been identified except for two Koreans mentioned earlier and a solitary Japanese who had related her experiences in a broadcast in 1986. Others had preferred to conceal their past shame, particularly those who had managed to achieve a more or less settled family life.

Now the issue became highly public and political. Soon after President Roh's visit, a socialist Diet member put a question in the Upper House as to whether comfort women had been included in the labor draft. He had been alerted to this possibility by recently published sources in Fuji Publishing Company's *Key Document Series on the Fifteen Year War*. The Director-General of the Employment Security Office, which held most of the relevant records, replied that they were not involved as they had 'just been taken around with the forces by private operators' without official involvement.

When this exchange became known in South Korea, it provoked a strong reaction among women's groups. Such groups, in the new climate of democratization more favorable to political activism, had for some years been agitating against sex tours from Japan and prostitution around U.S. bases, both regarded by the authorities as valuable sources of foreign exchange. They had come to realize that the comfort women issue, simultaneously shocking from the standpoints of morality, feminism, and patriotism, could be used to arouse strong emotions favorable to their general program, as sex tours and base prostitution could be portrayed as a perpetuation of the wartime practice. So they addressed an open letter to Prime Minister Kaifu demanding that the facts of the comfort women system be exposed, survivors or their families compensated, and that an account of the system be included in historical education.

The Japanese government, however, continued to deny official complicity or knowledge of the system and legal action was not possible in the absence of any surviving comfort women who would act as litigants. The breakthrough came in August 1991 when Kim Hak-sun, who had been forced into prostitution by Japanese forces in China, agreed to testify. She had lost her husband and children and could therefore cause them no shame. She was soon joined by two others, though these remained anonymous, and all three participated in a class action launched in the Tokyo District Court on 6 December 1991, the day before the 50th anniversary of the attack on Pearl Harbor. The lawsuit also included 11 ex-soldiers, five represented by their bereaved families, and 21 former paramilitary, including 11 represented by bereaved families. Six other former comfort women later joined the list of plaintiffs. A notional claim was laid of ¥20 million each, with a demand for an official apology from the Japanese government.

The Sakhalin lawsuit had been resumed the previous year, and in the previous month still another had been instituted by Korean ex-servicemen convicted and punished by allies for class B and C war crimes, for which they claimed compensation from the Japanese government as ultimately responsible. A little earlier a group of ex-paramilitary had lodged a claim in the district court at Osaka, center of the main concentrations of Koreans in Japan—a pattern repeated over succeeding years in various courts by a great variety of litigants of various nationalities.

Documentary evidence of official complicity in the comfort women system was initially lacking, but this was soon remedied in January 1992 by Professor Yoshimi Yoshiaki of Chuo University. He had long been carrying out research in the library of the national Institute for Defense Studies and, apart from various articles, had in 1987 published *Grass Roots Fascism,* which linked wartime psychology to the general modern Japanese contempt for other Asians. He had also co-authored a collection of documents on gas warfare. Hearing of the lawsuit involving the comfort women, he remembered noticing original wartime documents relating to the subject in the library and promptly retrieved five of them. Summaries of these were published at once in the *Asahi* morning edition of 11 January, and its evening edition already carried an admission from government spokesmen that 'deep involvement by the forces of the time cannot be denied.'

As Prime Minister Miyazawa was due to visit South Korea in only five days' time, he was interviewed before departure by South Korean media and expressed his regret and apologies in the strongest terms. He repeated this in the National Assembly and promised to produce an official report after a thorough search for evidence. His government maintained, however, that there was no legal basis for litigation as all South Korean claims against Japan arising from colonization and the war were explicitly described as settled by the terms of the Normalization Treaty of 1965. As an alternative, the authorities began to explore the possibility of a privately based Fund 'in lieu of compensation' along the lines of that established for atomic bomb victims in Korea. The litigants, however, rejected such a solution and the lawsuit continued, in the usual manner of such cases in Japan, for a number of years.

From the beginning it received worldwide coverage and continued to do so, while numerous other claimants emerged from several countries, notably the Philippines, where Japanese forces had either induced or coerced local women into sexual service. The issue eventually reached the United Nations Commission on Human Rights, while other lawsuits were taken up by Western former prisoners or internees. A great volume of additional documentation on comfort women was unearthed from Japanese archives. The promised Japanese official report contained 127 Japanese documents and Professor Yoshimi published a collection of 106 under the title *Reference Material for Military Comfort Women,* with an analysis, in 1992. Further testimony was also obtained from ex-servicemen via hotlines set up by women's organizations. Regarding the question of compensation, a majority of the respondents in the Tokyo area favored it, though only a minority in the Osaka area did so.

The impact within Japan was considerable and triggered a vigorous debate, notably in the *Asahi*'s letter columns. There was fairly widespread support for compensation. From an academic: 'As I listened to these expressions of apology, I could not help inwardly shouting How late! Really too late!... I reflected on the fate of many Korean women who had passed away during this too long gulf.' (Hicks 1995)

From a veteran on the China front:

> It is natural that rancor should penetrate their very marrow as a result of being physically ravaged in their youth. However, it cannot be said that all were drafted by the military. There were also operators who did business by assembling comfort women; some were Koreans and Chinese. There were also women who themselves became comfort women for money.... In any case, I think it appropriate that some kind of compensation should be made to the comfort women whose youth, never to return, was soiled on the battlefield. (Hicks 1995)

There was of course opposition too. From a retiree:

> If a haphazard investigation is made, it will produce new injustices, and there will be a limitless torrent of claims for compensation. It will not stop at China or Korea, but doubtless claims will be made from far-flung countries in Southeast Asia and the South Pacific. (Hicks 1995)

This practical argument was doubtless a factor in government thinking, though of course not openly admitted. A more psychological argument:

> The comfort women problem from the past, which seems to have been abruptly thrust upon us by South Korea, with demands for compensation from the national level, imparts a sense among us, as we are putting forth our best efforts for the present and future society, of being subject to 'psychological aggression.' (Hicks 1995)

On 4 August 1993, the very last day of the LDP's long grip on power, when defections had forced a transfer of power to an opposition coalition including the Socialist and (Buddhist) Clean Government Parties, the government issued a brief supplementary report conceding official involvement not only in operating the comfort system but in recruiting for it by means including deception and intimidation. This did not, however, bring either a political or a legal solution. The ensuing political instability inhibited difficult decisions, while the lawsuits continued, still hampered by the 1965 Normalization Treaty and other similar agreements. An Asian Women's Fund was raised from private contributions with the idea of offering a solatium in lieu of compensation, but the amount collected fell short of expectations and the litigants persisted in rejecting this solution, even if accompanied by an apology. Only the Sakhalin laborers' claim was settled, by a political initiative.

Mounting confrontations

Although Hayashi Fusao's *Affirmation of the Greater East Asian War* had caused a stir at the time of its publication, it did not at that stage stimulate any significant current of right wing revisionism. Japan was so well adjusted to its Cold War role and so successful in the pursuit of economic development that there was little inclination to embrace such a discordant theme. Hayashi's thesis was only raised sporadically in isolated contexts, but under Nakasone as prime minister, neonationalist revisionism gained some momentum and over the change of decade became more prominent. Even as the resurrection of Japan's war record was being pursued from abroad, revisionism intensified at home.

78

To a large extent this was defensive, but various factors were at work. Increasing economic tensions with the United States and the latter's frequent 'Japan-bashing' marked the end of Cold War symbiosis, and a natural corollary, for those who were historically minded, was to attack the U.S. view of the war as enshrined in the Tokyo trials. As one revisionist put it, Japan's real unconditional surrender was not that made to the Potsdam Declaration, which was tacitly conditional on the retention of the Emperor system, but was rather the subsequent surrender to the U.S. view of the war. Ideologically oriented elements deplored the manner in which principle had been subordinated to politics and economics in the Cold War alliance with the U.S.

The right wing was also heartened by the collapse of the Soviet bloc and the Tiananmen massacre, with the resulting decline in morale of the Japanese left wing and an overall shift to conservatism in the political spectrum. The Gulf War, with the dispatch of Self Defense mine sweepers and the later passage of the Peace Keeping Operations law, allowing the dispatch of forces overseas for such operations under United Nations auspices, strengthened arguments for constitutional revision. Significant overall for the molding of public opinion was the comparative sophistication and articulateness of some exponents of revisionist views, as compared with Germany and other Western countries where the extreme right is generally marginalized. Although professional historians tend either to Marxism or scholarly detachment, the 'nationalist intellectuals' include academics in other fields, some teachers, amateur historians, journalists, TV commentators, columnists, and popular lecturers. These have sometimes produced arguments plausible enough and with occasional factual basis to lend confidence to less sophisticated or cautious spokesmen or agitators. Details of some of the arguments raised will be studied in a later chapter.

In terms of content, revisionism has tended to move away from Hayashi's line, emphasizing liberation from Western imperialism, to the extent that it is perceived that the countries actually liberated generally show little gratitude to Japan. Growing knowledge of the conduct of the war has also made it clearer that the immediate aim of Japanese occupation was more a matter of exploitation than liberation or 'co-prosperity.' An authoritative expression of Japanese priorities is contained in the 'Principles for the administration of southern occupied areas' laid down by the high command at the outset of hostilities in December 1941. Relevant points are:

> (1) For the present a military administration will be established in the occupied areas for purposes of the restoration of order, the rapid acquisition of key defense resources and self-sufficiency of operational forces.... (7) Pressures on local living conditions unavoidable for the acquisition of defense resources and local self-sufficiency for occupation forces will be made to be endured and demands for placatory measures

will be limited to the extent not conflicting with the above objectives [a clear indication of the hardships that were to follow!].

Revisionism therefore now took as its point of departure the criticism of the 'Tokyo Trial view of history,' condemned as 'masochistic' by Nakasone and succeeding ideologues. As noted earlier, there are some quite objective grounds, recognized by many outside Japan too, for questioning the conduct of the trials themselves, but criticism presents problems for conservative revisionists. Most importantly, defenders of the Emperor as free from war responsibility had habitually quoted his exemption from prosecution as proof that the allies had accepted their view, so the right wing did not wish to question the trial procedures in such a way as to expose him to renewed blame. More broadly, analysis of the 'bargain' concluded between the occupation and the establishment could easily develop into an attack on the latter's role and responsibility.

From this the argument shifts to an emphasis on ambiguities in the character of the war. One of these was the tension felt in Japan's dual role as both the hegemon and the liberator of Asia, the former aspect relating to the war against China and the latter to the war against the Western colonial powers. As it is expressed in *The Greater East Asia War as seen from the End of the Century* (1991): 'Liberation and hegemony—this ambiguous character expresses the difficult task borne by Asia's first modern state which had to traverse the course of modernization amid conflict and confusion between Asianism and Westernization.' (Yoshida 1995)

Critics of course can point out that a mechanical separation of the two wars is unreal, in that the extension of the China war by the move into Indochina led to the clash with the Western powers. A greater ambiguity was Japan's maintenance of its own colonial empire in Korea, Taiwan, and southern Sakhalin along the same lines as the Western empires, without any suggestion that the status of these possessions was to be altered by the war, though a belated legislative decision was taken in 1944 to grant them equality under the then Constitution.

Further analysis beyond the distinction between the war's dual aspects tended to blame Japan's wartime leadership not for their moral responsibility but for their inadequacies in failing to cope with or comprehend the complexities of international politics in the 1930s, so ultimately being trapped between the intrigues of the Comintern, the Chinese communists, and President Roosevelt (who has been portrayed even in the West as having maneuvered Japan into attacking Pearl Harbor as the only means of overcoming isolationist opposition to involvement in the war in Europe). This, of course, is still war responsibility, if of a different kind.

A further trend in this direction is to an at least equal apportionment of blame between Japan and the United States. This seems to have penetrated fairly widely in public opinion, judging by a survey in November 1991 when

80

56 percent of the respondents laid blame on both equally, 30 percent on Japan solely and 4 percent on the US solely (presumably considering only the oil embargo). Curiously 1 percent replied that neither was to blame, which recalls the tendency in textbook screening to use neutral expressions, such as 'war breaking out' rather than an active 'making war.'

This survey was of course restrictive in excluding consideration of the roles of other powers, either Allied or Axis, so remaining tied to the 'Pacific War' orientation. Other revisionists broaden the spread of blame away from Japan to cover the whole perceived pattern of encirclement which was described in the lead-up to the war as 'ABCD,' meaning America, Britain, China, and Dutch East Indies, which ensured the completeness of the oil embargo. More broadly, the argument is sometimes extended to depict Japan as just one participant in the long-established pattern of worldwide interimperialist power struggles. Here the U.S. intervention in the Sino-Japanese conflict is seen not as undertaken for China's sake but merely using China's plight as a pretext in pursuing America's own drive to world hegemony. In this context, the locus of responsibility becomes most diffuse. In the last resort, however, the war can still be represented as having, in effect if not by design, 'contributed to the independence of Asian nations.'

The gradual rise of such revisionist debate emboldened more public figures to avow views of this sort openly. Education Minister Fujio's indiscretion of 1986 was followed a couple of years later by that of Okuno Seisuke, Director-General of the Land Agency and former Kempei. He rebuked China for describing Japan as an aggressor, claiming that Japan had been forced into a contest for supremacy by the Western powers. He was obliged to resign after Chinese protests but remained a chief mobilizer of revisionist sentiment in the LDP.

Then, in October 1990, Ishihara Shintaro, a former Minister of Transport, said in an interview with the U.S. magazine *Playboy* that the Nanking massacre was a Chinese fabrication. He had been a popular novelist and was a focus of right wing ideology in the LDP, where he had formed a grouping called the Spring Breeze Society to press for change rather on the lines of fellow-novelist Mishima but with less romanticism. He had also co-authored a best-selling book *The Japan that Can say No,* urging firm resistance to U.S. Japan-bashing on economic issues. The *Playboy* interview drew a strong protest from Chinese academics in the United States, but Ishihara reiterated the same line for the Japanese edition in the following month. Among other things, he also asserted that pistols and machine guns could not compare with atomic bombs in the level of atrocity, especially considering the long-term effects of radiation sickness. Although deaths were a concomitant of war, he was sure that anything like the scale claimed for Nanking by the Chinese (put at 300,000 deaths since their rediscovery of the issue in 1982) was a fabrication.

This brought widespread reaction within Japan too, notably from Honda Katsuichi, author of the early *Travels in China* which had initiated systematic studies on the massacre. He immediately challenged Ishihara with special persistence in the pages of the *Asahi Journal*. In his first article he reproduced the text of a registered letter he had sent to Ishihara, enclosing a reply envelope, demanding he reply within one month giving his grounds for denying the truth of the massacre. He followed this up over the next couple of months with other pieces in the *Journal* and the *Asahi* presenting the results of more recent research on the massacre.

In one article he quoted the research of a young businessman living in Fukushima Prefecture, north of Tokyo, named Ono Kenji. Over four years he had gathered data from his own locality on the war record of the 65th Regiment recruited there. His method was to unearth surviving war diaries and trace individuals mentioned in them. He had found over 200, of whom about 120 provided diaries or oral accounts of the Nanking campaign. He had arrived at figures for prisoners killed by this regiment along the Yangtze which closely approximated the 14,777 reported as captured by this unit in contemporary news sources at the time of the city's fall. They had been executed over two days by machine gun, the corpses being either burned with petrol or cast into the river. Diary entries mentioned two lots of 3,000 shot and 20,000 'disposed of,' with some Japanese also killed or wounded as a result of confusion when some prisoners broke away. The precise implication of the term 'disposed of' has sometimes been debated here and elsewhere, but Ono states that there is no mention anywhere of prisoners being released. Some entries described the disposal of corpses in the river.

A reader of this article brought Honda the diary of a deceased family member covering the period of the Nanking massacre. This recorded the capture of 17,025 prisoners over a few days, whom the unit was ordered to 'dispose of appropriately' as they could not be fed, which would require about 100 sacks of rice daily at a time when the Japanese themselves were subsisting by 'requisitioning.' Five soldiers are later mentioned as detailed to 'execute (explicitly) the remaining 10,000 or more.' Others then had to be sent to finish the task in a freezing night under a blizzard, while two more details of 25 and 15 were needed over the next two days to dispose of the corpses. In publishing the text of the entries, Honda omitted all names to spare his informant or others harassment by right wing 'Nanking massacre deniers.' He adds that the researchers are the true patriots who wish to spare Japan the international ridicule brought upon it by pseudopatriotic deniers.

In another article, Honda summarized material on Nanking becoming available from former East German archives. It consisted of reports from German embassy staff remaining in Nanking after most had departed with the retreating Nationalist government. A report dated February 1938 indicated that killings were still occurring nearly two months after the city's fall. Among other comments:

It seems that some time will be needed before senior Japanese officers succeed in halting the barbarities committed by units under their
command which have continued until the present.... It seems more important to them to dally with geisha than to observe their traditional
bushido code. (Honda 1991)

Also sent was documentary film taken by Father John Magee (who later
testified at the Tokyo trials) to be shown to Hitler. Honda wondered if this
material inspired Hitler to undertake the Holocaust, though such outside encouragement hardly seems needed. Most of the film is now lost, but a remaining portion shows the corpses of a Chinese Muslim family with an accompanying explanation that they had been murdered on the day of Nanking's
fall after the rape of the female members. The report mentions that, although
the international safety zone was spared much damage, abductions for the
purpose of rape had occurred there. It also relates General Matsui's expression
of regret in February to representatives of the Safety Zone Committee, and the
writer of the report expresses concern that the conduct of the Japanese troops
would foster Communist leanings among the Chinese. The Japanese Nanking
Incident Research Association regarded these materials as a valuable addition
to the multivolume *Reference Material on the Nanking Massacre Incident,*
which it had begun publishing in the mid-1980s.

As Ishihara had not replied within the month specified, Honda sent a re-
minder which brought a reply to the effect that in the *Playboy* interview, Ishihara's real intent had not been properly conveyed because of difficulties of
interpreting. For his precise views he referred Honda to a magazine article he
had written entitled 'The Scandal of the Information Vacuum that entrapped
Japan.' On examination, this included an attack on Honda accusing him of
fabricating sources but gave no clear grounds for Ishihara's own position.
Honda followed up by questioning Ishihara's allegation of faulty interpreting,
which could not apply to the Japanese edition. He demanded to be told where
the fault of interpreting lay and whether Ishihara had checked the proofs of the
Japanese, as he should, being a professional writer. He does not seem to have
replied directly, though a month or so later he wrote a more elaborate piece in
another journal portraying Japan as having being cornered into the ABCD encirclement and forced into war.

The next major occasion when Ishihara, as well as a wide spectrum of conservative opinion, emerged into public controversy was provided by the
statement from the first non-LDP prime minister Hosokawa, in a press conference on 10 August 1993, that 'I personally regard it as a war of aggression, a
mistaken war.' Although Ienaga as well as others recognized this stance as
largely promoted by interests concerned with avoiding friction in Asian relations, he conceded that it was something of an advance. Conservatives on the
other hand were incensed. Hosokawa's own Vice-Minister of Education, belonging to the rightward leaning Democratic Socialist Party, declared that

'responsibility was shared with America and Britain, in that Japan was cornered, and that it was not a matter of unilateral aggression.'

A couple of days later, in the War Dead Commemoration Day ceremony, Hosokawa, for the first time in such ceremonies, expressed regret for war victims other than Japanese in the words: 'I would like to take this opportunity to express deep condolences to victims of the war and their relatives in neighboring countries in Asia and those around the world.' This only widened the chorus of dissent. Being the occasion that it was, protests came particularly from the Japanese Association of War Bereaved Families. An LDP affiliated chairman of a council for Yasukuni Shrine matters addressed a demand for retraction to the Cabinet Chief Secretary with the words: 'Did those who died in that war die a pointless death? I wish the feelings of bereaved families to be considered.'

A meeting of cabinet members soon afterwards persuaded Hosokawa to tone down his position. He assured the meeting that he regarded the compensation issue as having been settled at the national level and in his subsequent Diet policy speech 'aggressive war' was modified to 'aggressive acts' in the words: 'Once again I express my feelings of profound self-reflection and apology for the unbearable suffering and sorrow occasioned to so many by our country's past aggressive acts and colonial rule.' With the usual sensitivity of critics to nuances, this was seen as a retreat, although the inclusion of an apology for colonialism was rather new.

An opinion survey held after his initial press conference generally favored his stand. Of respondents, 50 percent believed that the war was an aggressive one, 9 percent that it was largely so, 8 percent that it was not much so, and 8 percent that it was not so. Another survey held soon afterwards on compensation found that 34 percent regarded it as necessary, 21 percent as necessary to a certain extent, 9 percent as not very necessary, and 20 percent as not necessary.

Hosokawa's most active critic was of course Ishihara, now a member of the LDP in opposition. In an attack on the prime minister in a Lower House Budget Committee session in October, he took an analytical approach, dividing the war into three distinct aspects. These were: the war against China, the war against the Western powers maintaining colonies in southeast Asia, and the war launched by the Soviet Union against Japan in the final phase. This last he described as clearly aggression by the Soviet Union. The war against China had arisen, he claimed, from disputes over Japanese treaty rights acquired legally in terms of international law as understood at the time. Regarding the war against the Western powers 'who intruded on Asia with the same colonialism as Japan,' he compared this on a moral level to a territorial dispute between Yakuza gangs:

We have no need whatever to entertain apologetic sentiments towards Holland, France, America or Britain just because we lost. It is quite ludicrous—as both sides were guilty of the same offense, there is no point in comparing which side bears the heavier or lighter guilt. (Yoshida 1995)

It is of course hardly consistent to regard colonial type treaty rights in China as 'legal' while colonialism in Southeast Asia is an 'offense.' Regarding the earlier annexation of Korea, he remarked that, if Japan had not annexed that country, 'in view of the anarchy in Korea at that time it would certainly have been annexed by neighboring Manchu China or Russia,' which at least agrees with the British view in concluding the Anglo-Japanese alliance at that time. This outburst did not cause international repercussions as Ishihara was in opposition.

Reactions outside the Diet continued. Comments on the Commemoration Day speech from the Association of Shinto shrines in the organ *Shrine News*, while conceding that Japan's initial aim in the incursion into Southeast Asia was to secure resources, also claimed that it simultaneously embodied the 'grand ideal of the liberation of the Orient.' Later, regarding Hosokawa's policy speech, it claimed that Japan's colonialism had 'a constructive, positive side in enormous investment, increased means of production and education'— the same claim, true only in a certain sense, as was often made for other colonial empires.

An organization called The National Committee to Deny that Japan is an Aggressor placed a full page advertisement in the conservative *Sankei* attacking Hosokawa and followed this up with a 'national rally to censure the Hosokawa cabinet' in the Japan Industrial Club. This passed a resolution condemning the 'masochistic view of history' which called for the retraction of Hosokawa's statement and was conveyed to the government by Fujio, who was still a Diet member. The advertisement, which gave as the committee's contact point a body called the New Japan Council, took a Question and Answer format which sketches much of the scope of revisionist argument, along the lines:

Q: Is it proper to pass judgment on a past war in the form of a parliamentary resolution or government statement?

A: There is no example of this being done anywhere in the world [critics quote Germany as an example, though probably the only one].

Q: Does Japan still owe reparations arising out of the war?

A: Except for North Korea, with which we have no diplomatic relations, all have been settled at the national level.

Q: In the preceding world war, did Japan make war on Southeast Asian countries?

A: What Japan fought was the domination of the Western powers that had colonized Southeast Asia.

85

Q: Prime Minister Hosokawa stated that Japan waged an aggressive war but exactly what sort of war is meant?

A: It was only 19 years ago that provisional international agreement was reached on the definition of aggression.

Q: In the matter of war responsibility, Japan and Germany are often compared, but was the situation the same in both countries?

A: Japan cannot be classed with Nazi Germany, which suspended its constitution and parliament and deliberately planned aggressive war.

Q: What were the Tokyo Trials that treated Japan as an aggressor?

A: They were merely part of occupation policy for which the victor assumed the guise of a trial. (Tawara 1995)

This was followed a few months later by another full page advertisement in *Sankei* inserted by the Association to Recognize Fallen Heroes, which included the Shrine and Bereaved Families Associations, under the heading 'Japan is not an Aggressor. Our fallen heroes were not accomplices in aggressive war.'

The next major indiscretion at the government level was committed in May 1994 by Nagano Shigeto, Minister of Justice in the succeeding Hata cabinet, who had previously been Chief of Staff of the Ground Self Defense Forces. Immediately after the cabinet was formed, he declared in a political meeting that the Nanking massacre was a fabrication and that the Pacific War was not one of aggression on Japan's part. He also was obliged to retract, apologize, and resign.

Hata himself, however, marked a further retreat from Hosokawa's initial position. To a question by a member of the Socialist Party, which had deserted the coalition from being denied an acceptable role in its power structure, Hata replied:

I also recognize that aggressive acts occurred in relation to the war. Actually the significance of the term and usage 'aggressive war' is not clearly established. However, when I reflect on it, aggressive acts certainly occurred as an effect of it.... Reflecting on this, we are now facing fifty years since the war and frankly apologize to all who have suffered. (Yoshida 1995)

This position is described as 'aggression in effect' as a definition falling somewhat short of the implications of deliberate or planned aggression. A Communist party member later pressed the distinction, pointing out that 'aggressive acts' might merely indicate isolated acts of indiscipline that were not a matter of official policy, as would be implied by 'aggressive war.' Hata merely replied that he himself, unlike the questioner, was not the type of person to pursue points so academically.

At the same time, the *Sankei* ran a series of studies on the war with a revisionist slant. For this purpose it set up a 'Fifty years postwar viewpoint committee.' The resulting series was entitled 'An investigation: the Condemnatory View of History,' this last term being introduced as an improvement on the usual 'masochistic view.' It focused on 'the independence of countries and Japan's role.' It did allow some debate between a writer of clearly revisionist bent and a professional historian who described the war as 'defensive' only in the sense of defending Japan's domination of China and Korea, but editorial opinion regarding the correct name for the war rejected 'Pacific War' as being characteristic of 'devotees of the Tokyo Trial view,' recognizing only the alternative 'Greater East Asia War,' rather than the now widely preferred 'Asia-Pacific War.'

These high level admissions of aggression did however meet a positive response in some quarters, notably in the best known regional center of war commemoration—the Hiroshima Peace Memorial Museum. Previously, this had only displayed the effects of the atomic bomb with just the briefest reference to the attack on Pearl Harbor as background to the bombing. But in mid-1994, it was recast with much fuller coverage of Japan's provocations, including a display on the Nanking massacre, with a picture of citizens of Hiroshima celebrating that city's fall with a lantern parade, as then customary to build war morale. American motives for using the bomb are listed with some balance, including the desire to test a new weapon, to restrict allied casualties to a minimum, and to forestall Soviet intervention. Objections were, however, encountered, such as that from the Secretary-General of the Atomic Bomb Victims Association, who declared 'Japan was certainly involved in wars in Asia as an oppressor, but that is one thing and the atomic bomb is another'—a further case of the distinction between aspects of the war.

Similar reaction on a smaller scale later occurred in the corresponding museum to the second atomic bomb attack in Nagasaki. An attempt at balance had been made by devoting a corner to an illustrated chronological chart of the history of Japan's expansionism and related wars. The Nanking massacre was originally illustrated by a photograph of a woman being harassed by Japanese troops, but protests were lodged by a Citizens Association to Rectify the Nagasaki Atomic Bomb Museum, partly on the grounds of anachronism in the troops' equipment. This is not impossible because photographs used in war propaganda can sometimes be of dubious origin. It was therefore replaced by a photograph of refugees leaving Nanking, though without any details as to their reason for flight. The Association still objected, however, on more general grounds, particularly that such material might lead 'naive schoolchildren' to conclude that the bomb was justified. In their view, too, the Nanking massacre was a separate issue from the atomic bomb.

Reaction and fictionalization

The Hata Cabinet was crippled from the start by the desertion of the Socialists who soon combined with the rump LDP to overthrow it. Such a coalition between the major conservative and reformist parties seems paradoxical from the standpoint of Western political processes but in the Japanese context seems just another example of the frequently noted dominance of pragmatism over theory. To obtain a clear majority, however, support was needed from the smaller Harbinger Party (Sakigake) which insisted that the Socialists' leader Murayama Tomiichi be prime minister. In recognition of the weight carried by the LDP, however, the party abandoned long-held socialist principles by recognizing the Self Defense Forces as constitutionally legal, as well as their dispatch overseas for peace keeping purposes, and approved the official use of the national anthem and flag. These had been treated as militaristic symbols, though they long pre-dated the era of political dominance by the military. They are, of course, monarchistic, but this is not a live issue, except to the Communists to some extent.

The mood of compromise also affected the Japan Teachers' Union. Tension with the Education Ministry and conservative Diet members had been easing from both sides simultaneously. On its side, the Union's membership had been steadily falling along with the general decline in the left wing, until it embraced only 34 percent of teachers, as compared with a peak of 80 percent. On the other side, the education policy grouping of Diet members had lost much of its cohesion amid complex party splits and general instability. The Education Ministry in its turn, being both freed from these pressures and influenced by high-level war apologies, reflecting the need to conciliate Asian opinion, came to allow a substantial degree of freedom in textbook treatment of the war. Relevant portions of the resulting improved texts were then published in English, Chinese, and Korean translations by the Foreign Ministry as part of its overall strategy of eliminating the textbook issue as an obstacle to Asian relations. Details will be discussed later.

Nevertheless the new cabinet still produced its share of controversy on views of the war. Murayama himself, in the spirit of coalition consensus, avoided the term 'aggressive war' in favor of 'aggressive acts' in his Diet policy speech, though in his first press conference he spoke of 'the need to reflect fully and humbly on Japan's responsibility in occasioning such great calamities.' More serious, however, was the next major indiscretion, this time by Sakurai Shin, Minister for the Environment. In a meeting in August 1994, he asserted that the war was not one of aggression or one for which Japan was solely responsible, also emphasizing Japan's role in the independence of Asian nations and their subsequent prosperity. Protests forced his resignation.

Yet again, however, only a couple of months later, Hashimoto Ryutaro, Minister of International Trade and Industry, stated in the Diet itself that although there were aspects in relations with China and Korea on which aggression could not be denied, the case of the Greater East Asia War, fought against the Western powers, was different. 'To me, it is doubtful whether it could be described as aggressive war.' But his political position was much stronger than that of others who had suffered from such statements, as he was the head of the Bereaved Families Association and held a crucial position in the tense trade confrontations with the United States, in which he proved unusually successful. Murayama took no action against him, and he ultimately came to lead the governing coalition as Prime Minister in 1996.

Revisionist views of this kind do border on fantasy at times, though some subjectivity is inevitable in any historical interpretation. Beyond this, however, outright and deliberate fantasy was becoming a major feature in what passed for war literature in this period, amounting to what one critic describes as a 'flight from history.' Even within this area, though, there are degrees of fantasy. The category described as 'simulation war novels' is closer to reality in that it deals with actual situations that arose during the war and hypotheses on the results that might have followed from alternative key decisions or more or less fortuitous variables, generally with outcomes favorable to Japan. Although this category tends to glorify war, it does not try to whitewash the nature and behavior of the Japanese forces, and it can be treated as a type of historical analysis by comparing the effects of various scenarios.

The pioneer in this treatment of the war was Hiyama Yoshiaki's *Decisive Battle for the Japanese Homeland* (1991), which explored the possibilities that last-ditch strategists had envisaged before the atomic bomb attacks. One recent publication of this kind which, though from a revisionist perspective, amounts to a fairly informative exercise in historical analysis is *This is how the Pacific War could have been won* (1995). It consists of a dialogue between two academics, with high qualifications mainly in the field of economics. In the introduction one of them outlines the types of scenarios used in simulation studies along these lines:

> What if there had been a difference of five minutes—a different commander—different weapons used—better preparation—three different words in the operation order—new weapons developed in time? Questions arise as: why were deficient weapons not replaced—deficient staff not replaced—deficient intelligence trusted? (Kusaka 1995)

Even such a treatment as this, from hindsight, can divert readers from reality but much more so a second category recently becoming highly successful, described as 'entertainment' or 'fictional' war novels. In these, for example, imaginary weapons are used and the conduct of the forces unrealistically idealized. The most notable example is the *Sapphire Fleet* series by Aramaki Yoshio, beginning in 1991, which became a major best seller at over three million copies. Over 1993-94 all types of this genre accounted for over half the paperback sales of *Chuo Koron* publications, amounting to over four million copies and over 60 titles. A 1995 survey found that such publications had so far reached 150 titles and 250 volumes.

As to the ideological slant, even the more realistic Hiyama described his writing in 1993 as 'a reaction and challenge to the postwar so-called progressive intellectuals who speak only of being antiwar. I hope by adopting the guise of entertainment, to revise the Tokyo Trial view of history treating Japan as wholly at fault.' Aramaki goes still further in speaking of 'making a psychoanalysis of the Japanese race,' though inverting what the Japanese forces actually did. Prisoners are released and Japan withdraws from the mainland after completing the task of 'liberation;' even fighting in expectation of defeat as a sacrifice for the ideal. The conduct of the forces is always strictly correct.

Much of such material also takes the form of comics, and the whole vogue has also fed into that of simulator games on home computers, where the game is all that matters and questions of guilt or propriety are utterly irrelevant. To a defense that 'it doesn't matter because it's just a game,' a critic replies: 'it's wrong just because it's a game.' Complete amorality is even more dangerous than revisionism which at least argues from principle. This phenomenon is not of course by any means peculiar to Japan.

The Diet's Fiftieth War-End Anniversary resolution

On taking office in July 1994 Prime Minister Murayama, in wording agreed on by the three-party coalition, promised that by the 50th anniversary of the war's end in the following year, the Diet would pass a resolution of 'self-criticism for Japan's aggressive acts and colonial rule.' The Japanese term *hansei* used here, which is most accurately rendered as 'self-criticism' or perhaps 'self-reproach,' has customarily been rendered in English as 'remorse' or 'reflection,' but the former is too strong and the latter too weak. The more accurate equivalent tends to be avoided as unfamiliar in English usage, though common in East Asian contexts, but it is best kept for the purpose of conveying as closely as possible the nuances of debates surrounding it. A Diet resolution was felt to be essential, and was especially urged by South Korea, as representing the expression of the nation as a whole, as distinct from the more individual apologies made by the new Emperor and several prime ministers.

To prepare for this and related measures the government set up a 'Committee to Resolve Postwar Issues.' One of its functions was to organize two funds as a means of evading acceptance of the potentially astronomical claims for war compensation. The first fund, to cover the comfort women issue, was to be raised from private sources and to be called the 'Asia Peace and Friendship Fund for Women.' The second, the 'Peace, Friendship and Exchange Initiative,' was more official in character but essentially continued earlier policies of aid in lieu of reparations or compensation.

To frame a suitable Diet resolution, the coalition in due course set up a project team to arrive at a formula acceptable to all its component parties—by no means an easy task. It was also desirable that account be taken of other parties in the Diet to achieve a result that could be regarded as nationally comprehensive. The remaining components of the former anti-LDP coalition had meanwhile amalgamated into the New Frontier Party led by the former LDP prime minister Kaifu. This took an active interest in the resolution question, setting up its own project team, and initially considered drafting an alternative resolution, though this plan was ultimately dropped. Contacts between the coalition and the NFP were made through the Diet steering committee. There was also the Communist Party which could certainly be counted on to denounce Japan's colonial and war record in the strongest terms but naturally exceeding what any other parties would be likely to accept.

Even the more or less restrained terminology preferred by executives in the LDP and NFP brought rebellion in both camps. That in the LDP was rallied by Okuno Seisuke, earlier dismissed from government office for denying aggression in China, in the form of the 'Fiftieth War-End Anniversary Diet Members' League.' These opposed any reference to aggressive acts or colonization and sought to substitute a statement of mourning and resolution for peace. They came to account for something over two-thirds of LDP Diet members, though with varying degrees of commitment, who exerted considerable pressure on the party executives in toning down their draft resolution. In the NFP, too, a rebel group formed under the name 'Diet Members' League for conveying accurate history,' though these carried less weight than their LDP counterparts, largely because of their party's even more heterogeneous character.

Outside the Diet, the National Congress to safeguard Japan conducted a widely effective campaign to have local assemblies pass their own resolutions justifying the war or opposing an apologetic posture. The Bereaved Families Association gathered 4.56 million signatures for a rally on the Diet resolution held on 29 May 1995, timed to coincide with the Diet session when the resolution was to be moved. It was held at the Martial Arts Stadium with an attendance of 10,000. Okuno delivered the keynote address and was followed by a number of supporting speakers from Asian countries, notably Thailand, Indonesia, Cambodia, and India. These had been recruited to support his thesis that 'people in Asia were able to be liberated from colonial rule by the whites and achieved their independence' after 'Japan's war of self-defense against the ABCD encirclement.'

At the end of May, the government coalition were still far from reaching a consensus, while at the same time they regarded this as essential to preserve the coalition and avoid a Lower House election, in which the prospects were uncertain. Among the party drafts there was general agreement on a resolve to preserve peace and in particular work for the abolition of nuclear weapons, though only the Socialist and Harbinger drafts mentioned the Constitution. All

91

made some reference to accepting the lessons of history, though the Harbinger draft spoke in terms of Japan's involvement in interimperialist struggles from the 19th century, which tended to generalize blame. Only the Socialists specifically mentioned Korea, the labor draft, and comfort women. All included the theme of mourning for all war dead, though the LDP included some extra wording more specific to the sacrifice of Japanese dead for the fatherland. Only the Socialists mentioned an 'apology' but agreed with the Harbinger Party on a minimum of 'self-criticism for aggressive acts and colonization' as in Murayama's original undertaking. The LDP, under pressure from Okuno's grouping, were reluctant to agree to this, though Okuno's argument warning against harm to Japan's national interests was opposed by the party leadership on the grounds that securing international trust was paramount. Hashimoto, as president of the Bereaved Family's Association, presented the association's view that there was no objection to a peace resolution but that any wording humiliating to bereaved families must be avoided. The combined project team finally accepted the coalition's partners' wording here, as LDP leaders themselves had used such terms in the past, though it was toned down by a generalization on interimperialist guilt on the lines of the Harbinger draft.

The NFP opposition had prepared an alternative draft but, on further contact in the Diet steering committee, dropped the plan for a separate motion, being prepared to support an acceptable government draft and to issue its own draft as a party statement only. It included the theme of generalized interimperialist struggle which had involved Japan 'even if for self-preservation,' with a statement of thanks to countries that had supported Japan's development.

In the midst of these negotiations, a most discordant note was struck by Watanabe Michio, former foreign minister, who at a local LDP meeting denied that Japan's rule in Korea had constituted colonization and claimed that the treaty of annexation had been legal and concluded amicably. It is true that in formal terms the Korean royal house had signed the treaty and had been rewarded with high rank in the Japanese aristocracy, but this was only the culmination of years of Japanese intrigue and military-economic penetration. As a further argument, Watanabe pointed out that Japan's reconstruction aid for South Korea under the 1965 Normalization Treaty had not been described as reparations, as would have been applicable if Japan had been an invader. South Korean reactions were predictable enough, reviving earlier calls for the revision of the 1965 treaty to specify that Japan's occupation had always been illegal, as well as calling on Watanabe to die by *seppuku* in samurai fashion to expiate his offense.

On 5 June the government project team had still not settled the final wording of the draft resolution, so this was left to the executives of the three parties to be put to the Diet for passage not later than the end of the week on 9 June. The next day, the final agreed version was published, of which the official English read:

This Diet, in the fiftieth year since the war, offers its sincere tribute to the memory of the war dead throughout the world and victims who have suffered because of war and other deeds.

Recalling the many instances of colonial rule and acts of aggression in the modern history of the world, we recognize those acts which our country carried out and the unbearable suffering inflicted on the people of other countries, particularly the nations of Asia, and express deep remorse.

Transcending differences in historical view of the past war, we must humbly learn the lessons of history and build a peaceful international community.

This Diet links hands with the countries of the world under the doctrine of lasting peace enshrined in the Constitution of Japan and expresses its determination to open up a future of coexistence for humankind.

We affirm the above.

The term rendered 'remorse' was, as mentioned earlier, the Japanese *hansei,* more accurately meaning 'self-criticism,' though 'deep' strengthens it. The word 'unbearable' was not in the Japanese text, though it had been used earlier. The term rendered 'enshrined' more accurately reads 'proclaimed.' In the Japanese, however, 'such acts' rather than 'those acts' is somewhat clearer in intent.

When the NFP saw this draft, they felt unable to support it as it stood. It was objected that it was illogical to speak of 'learning the lessons of history' if there were still 'differences in historical view of the war,' since there needs to be agreement on what these lessons are. The party leader, however, overruled the dissenting faction who advocated outright rejection of the draft, in favor of an attempt at a negotiated amendment.

The NFP representatives on 9 June tried to persuade the government to delete 'transcending differences in historical view of the past war' and to add to that sentence 'particularly with the elimination of nuclear weapons,' as well as to add to the preceding second paragraph 'promising never again to repeat such acts.' The reference to nuclear weapons was acceptable as it had been in the coalition drafts and only dropped for simplicity as covered in 'lasting peace,' but the government representatives imposed a deadline of only ten minutes for acceptance or further argument by the NDP, so finally the whole of that party boycotted the Diet vote.

The resolution was therefore passed unaltered, under the title 'Resolution on the Lessons of History and renewed Resolve for Peace' but only by the members of the coalition who were in attendance, while the communists voted against it as 'ambiguous.' Apart from the NFP boycott, other absentees were 55 LDP, mainly hardliners of Okuno's faction including Watanabe, 14 Socialists, and 4 Harbinger members. Most of the two latter categories dissented from the weakened tone of the resolution, though some of the absentees from all parties were due to more fortuitous reasons. Some were detained elsewhere by official or party business, some were ill, and the Harbinger leader, who was also Finance Minister, was attending a staff member's wedding! Others had left for the day expecting that negotiations with the NFP would force a carryover to the following week.

The party's leader Kaifu was strongly critical of the government's failure to allow this in the interests of reaching a more representative consensus. As he put it: 'The fact that the ruling coalition rushed the matter proves that their draft was a brittle compromise that threatened to fall apart if left on the shelf for just one weekend.' He lodged a protest with the Speaker and Vice-Speaker of the Lower House on the grounds of breach of standard procedure.

It was generally recognized at home and abroad that the exercise had fallen short of its objective of broad reconciliation, as the number of members voting for the resolution was a minority of the total Diet membership, while ideally such a resolution should be unanimous. South Korean reactions were mildly favorable to the extent that aggression and colonization had been admitted but attacked the omission of a clear renunciation of war and a direct apology. Demonstrators threw eggs at the Japanese embassy and demanded Watanabe's execution.

Prime Minister Murayama, on the actual anniversary of the war's end, did utter a statement of apology along the lines of the Socialist's Party's draft, but this of course was not the equivalent of a Diet resolution. It was also undercut by a statement in the same month by Education Minister Shimomura Yoshinobu to the effect that it was not appropriate to speak of a war of aggression. He had to make a public apology. A few months later, too, the Director-General of the Management and Coordination Agency had to resign after stating that 'Japan did some good things for Korea during its colonial rule.'

A more significant development in the direction of revivalist nationalism was the government's final approval, after long debate, of the construction of a national war museum with public funds to amount to $120 million. It was to be run by the War Bereaved Families Association, its aim being, as expressed by the Welfare Ministry official in charge of the project, 'to collect, preserve and exhibit information about Japanese life during and after the war,' particularly the sufferings of families of war dead. To placate groups who had protested against the exclusion of Japan's war victims and attempted to block the museum's construction by legal action, he promised a more comprehensive future project which would include an Asian History Documentation Centre.

Constitutional amendment—some examples

As the final draft of the resolution had referred to the Constitution as the embodiment of Japan's peace ideal, it implicitly supported the preservation of Article 9, the most fundamental underlying purpose of the whole domestic movement to recognize Japan's war responsibility and expose its record. But the pressure for its amendment persisted even after the failure of the last major effort in that direction under Nakasone.

Without textual amendment, there had already been what is described as 'interpretative amendment' which, despite the prohibition of 'war potential,' progressively permitted the formation of the police reserve, the security force, and finally the Self Defense Forces to the extent of their overseas dispatch for U.N. peacekeeping operations. This last development was propelled by the Gulf War, which in turn strengthened arguments for textual amendment to eliminate persisting suggestions of legal anomaly.

Various grounds are raised, for example the shame that Japan's contribution to the Gulf War was 'blood tax (financial only) rather than blood,' that circumstances have changed completely since the Constitution was drafted, and that Japan's international role should include 'a military aspect to match its economic aspect.' One suggested approach has been, rather than alter the constitutional wording itself, to qualify Article 9 by a Basic Peace Law defining the character of a defense system restricted to the minimum.

A prominent proposal for verbal amendment was made by Ozawa Ichiro, the main power broker in the NFP, who in 1996 became its leader. Since his earlier period in the LDP before it lost power, he had been a consistent advocate of Japan's becoming a 'normal nation' with a military capability adequate to share in world leadership but strictly under the constitutional control that Japan's wartime leadership had defied. He had been the main mover in passing the Peace Keeping Operations bill through the Diet against the most determined opposition and in 1993 published a best-selling *Blueprint for a New Japan* in which he suggested adding a third paragraph to Article 9 to read:

> 3. The preceding paragraphs, however, do not impede the maintenance of Self Defense Forces acting for the securing of peace, the maintenance of a force available to the United Nations to act under its directions at its request or the activities of such a force under United Nations direction. (Rekishi Kyoikusha 1995)

A Basic Peace and Security Law under Article 9 to the same effect, Ozawa suggested, would be an alternative which was procedurally simpler.

A proposal for the abolition and replacement of Article 9 was made as part of comprehensive constitutional amendments drafted by *Yomiuri* in 1994. The new article would read:

Japan can possess an organization for self defense to safeguard its peace and independence and maintain its security.... On the basis of the preceding article Japan will cooperate positively in the activities of an established international structure. When necessary, it can dispatch public officials and provide part of its self defense organization for activities to maintain and promote peace and for humanitarian aid.

Another prominent advocate for such constitutional change has been Professor Fujioka Nobukatsu of Tokyo University, a focal figure for a group of like-minded LDP politicians. He has also written extensively on revisionist themes, both in articles in the *Sankei* and in several books which have sold well. One of these, entitled *History not Taught in the Textbooks*, sold over half a million copies in late 1996. It concentrates on episodes representing Japan's war as a legitimate reaction to Western expansionism and as having benefited Asia, using such examples as that of Japanese troops who remained in Indonesia after the war and contributed to its successful struggle for independence, earning President Soekarno's public thanks (as actually occurred).

Another book, *The Disgrace of Modern History,* disputes the coercive aspect of the comfort women system, claiming as the Japanese government originally did that such women were recruited under the contract system legally permitted in prewar Japan—which did apply in a proportion of cases but certainly not most. He also notes the existence of similar practices in other armies and naturally shares the usual revisionist aim of restoring national pride, advocating a return to the exclusion of material incompatible with this from textbooks. 'Writing only about Japan's faults is nonsensical. The Japanese are not a particularly noble people, but they are not obscene either.'

It is now argued that the Socialist Party's acceptance of the Self Defense Forces as constitutional has removed political obstacles to the amendment of Article 9. In tactical terms, up to the present, the left wing parties and Komeito have been enabled to deny proponents of constitutional revision the necessary two-thirds of both Diet houses to initiate a referendum, by virtue of the roughly proportional representation achieved by the traditional multimember constituency system. This system had the theoretical merit of ensuring the representation of a wide spectrum of interest groups without the extreme fragmentation likely in fully proportional representation. It did, however, produce evils of its own in complex factional struggles generating an intractable morass of corruption which eventually compelled reform.

The electoral law was accordingly amended to elect 60 percent of Lower House members from single seat constituencies, and in the October 1996, election conservative forces much increased their representation. The result was a wholly LDP government, though, being short of a clear majority, this depended on informal external support, which was received for lack of any viable alternative. Regarding elements opposed to constitutional amendment, Socialist Party representation fell to about half, partly through defections to a new Democratic Party, while the Communist Party outstripped it by nearly doubling its representation from winning over former Socialist supporters disillusioned with that party. Within the NFP, which declined slightly, the former Komeito grouping represents the solidest faction. With this lineup, however, proponents of constitutional revision, in the doubtful event that they could agree on a proposal, may well obtain enough support to put it to a referendum. This would provide a direct test as to how far the desire to preserve the peace constitution, with all its implications as to views of the Asia-Pacific War, is held by the population at large.

6 The evolution of textbook screening

For a number of years after the abolition of feudalism in the early 1870s, government policy on education was directed to the maximum diffusion in all fields of the modern knowledge needed for Japan's survival in the heyday of Western imperialism, so both official and private schools were allowed to use any material they regarded as suitable. But social development was so rapid and resulted in such ferment that the authorities as early as 1880 compiled a list of titles banned for use as textbooks because their content was too radical. Apart from this list, schools were only restricted by a system of reporting what texts were in use until in 1886 a system of prior certification of texts was introduced.

When a partially representative system of government was introduced with the 1889 Constitution, possible 'excesses' were to be counterbalanced by an education system focused on nationalist solidarity on the more conservative type of Western model (God, King, and Country), aimed both at promoting Japan's international ambitions and inhibiting radicalism at home. From 1904, primary school texts were produced by the Education Ministry itself, and, although secondary level texts retained the certification system until 1943, their contents were restricted by the closely prescribed curriculum. So, given this long background of educational controls, it is not surprising that, after a few years in the first flush of freedom under post-1945 liberal reform, earlier patterns steadily reemerged with the Cold War and 'reverse course.'

In 1946 a new departure was set in historical education with the issue of the textbook *Our Nation's Path,* prepared under occupation authority to replace the earlier ultranationalistic line centered on the Imperial House and mainly concerned with the deeds of statesmen and soldiers. In the same year, the Education Ministry's *Guide to New Education* stated: 'From the Manchurian Incident, Japan followed an undemocratic political and economic course at home and acted contrary to international legal and moral tenets abroad.... We must never repeat these mistakes.'

Historical education was incorporated in Social Studies to impart a more civic oriented treatment, and the new Basic Education Law of 1947 stated in its preamble that the realization of the ideals of the new Constitution 'must depend fundamentally on the power of education.' Its Article 10 forbade 'improper control of education'—meaning of the kind previously practiced. Under this policy, the Education Ministry issued non-restrictive 'draft guidelines' which explicitly rejected the previous 'mechanical, uniform' approach to education 'leading to the loss of creativity and initiative,' emphasizing that education must be adapted to local and individual needs.

To implement this policy, the following year saw the establishment of locally elected school boards for the autonomous supervision of education in each prefecture. Their role was described as 'not submitting to improper controls' but administering education suited to the actual conditions of each area. The teaching profession enthusiastically embraced its role within this framework and was organized in the nationwide Japan Teachers' Union, the largest such union in Japan. Unofficial educational associations also became active.

The writing and publication of textbooks were not subject to controls, their selection for use in teaching to be made at the school level after screening by the school boards. The main criteria for screening were suitability in regard to standards and local conditions and the exclusion of ultranationalistic ideology. The boards never effectively exercised this function, however, because of practical exigencies. An acute shortage of paper forced its surrender 'for the time being' to the Education Ministry, which in 1950 coordinated this activity in the Textbook Screening Research Council composed of academics and school administrators.

At this stage, the spirit of the Basic Law was still expected to prevail but before long the effects of the 'reverse course' came to be felt. The Teachers' Union from the start showed left wing and pacifistic tendencies as a reaction against earlier repression, and the authors of textbooks, then mainly academics, tended to produce material catering to such leanings, either in the hope of having their texts selected or out of conviction. So in 1951, with the Korean War at its height, Prime Minister Yoshida's Cabinet Orders Advisory Committee proposed a return to state production of texts, though opposition was strong enough to prevent this, then or even later.

The government's fallback position materialized in 1953 with amendments to the School education and School Board Laws permanently restricting the screening and authorization function to the Education Ministry. Arguments for centralized screening have included the need for nationwide equality of opportunity and uniform standards, accuracy, political neutrality, objective terminology, and simplification suited to the appropriate level. The supposed posture of neutrality was formulated the following year by the law enforcing political neutrality in education and the prohibition of political activity by teachers, both aimed at curbing left wing and pacifistic tendencies. It reflected the decision prompted by the Ikeda-Robertson talks to reorient education towards patriotism and defense consciousness, befitting Japan's role as 'bulwark against communism' in Asia.

A more positively reactionary trend appeared in 1955 in what is called 'the First "bias in textbooks" Attack,' an 'ominous turning point' marking the first coordinated onslaught on the educational scene by the education policy group of conservative Diet members. The Democratic party had made textbook standards an issue in its successful election campaign and later issued a pamphlet entitled 'The Deplorable Textbook Question,' charging the Teachers' Union with the promotion of 'red texts' and seeking public support for tougher screening. The next year, the now combined LDP government passed a law making the school boards appointive, though by local government and retaining administrative independence of the Education Ministry. A bill for the direct control of textbook content failed through factional differences, but a system of appointing textbook examiners by ministerial order evaded the need for special legislation, and a rush of disqualifications followed. At this stage, however, screening tended rather to the deletion of passages objected to than the later policy of indicating desired revisions. From 1957, however, the Federation of Publishing Employees' Unions began issuing its yearly 'Textbook Reports' which have continued to support the Teachers' Union with a thorough critical review of the operation of the screening system. Publishers, of course, have been placed between the two fires of Ministry examiners and textbook authors.

By 1958, all Course Guidelines were revised to be no longer 'draft' and the use of the curriculum to regulate screening became legally binding, rulings being issued through the Official Gazette and such channels. This formed the basis of the system elaborated and operating up to 1989, based on examiners' comments. These, as mentioned earlier, were divided into the two categories of mandatory 'corrections' and suggested 'improvements,' ultimately not mandatory if authors or publishers persisted. The former category related to 'demonstrable facts or views commonly accepted in works of an educational standard,' the latter to the more general standards of presentation mentioned earlier, such as political neutrality and objectivity. Regarding historical issues, for example, it was preferred to avoid 'negative, emotive or value-charged' terms in favor of what in practice tended to euphemism. Reasons for avoiding the term 'aggression' have been stated as follows:

> 'Aggression' is a term implying a negative value judgment and it is not desirable for the education of the nation's next generation to employ in textbooks terms implying a negative value judgment on the acts of one's own country, so an expression such as 'armed advance' should, for example, be employed. (Nik-Kan Rekishi Kyokasho Kenkyukai 1993)

The comments were explained orally by the examiner to the publisher or author who could tape-record or take notes, but the deliberations leading to the formulation of the comments were highly confidential ('in camera'), as were any subsequent negotiations between the examiner and those affected. The disclosure of some documentation on these proceedings was one achievement of Ienaga's litigation. Some examples of the style of the examiner's comments will be given later in the account of his lawsuits.

If the examiner produced no comments of either kind, the textbook was immediately qualified. If faults of content or production exceeded a certain level it would be automatically disqualified. In most cases, comments were made in terms of 'conditional qualification,' that is, conditional on the 'corrections' being made, with at least some attention to the 'suggestions.' There was no tight deadline for the submission of the revised text, but when this had been examined and passed, perhaps after further negotiations, a sample copy would be produced and, upon a final check, authorized for selection by the teaching authorities.

The next major extension of textbook control came with the introduction of cost-free primary and junior secondary texts in 1963. Although this arose from public demand, it is described as virtually achieving the effect of state production of texts without the degree of cost that this would entail. In the first place, publishers were limited to those meeting certain qualifications which included specified levels of capital, editorial staff, and publishing experience, as well as freedom from bankruptcy or criminal records.

Next, further limitations were imposed by the financial aspects of government policy, resulting in a narrow oligopoly. A system of uniform text selection over wide unit areas meant fewer titles with high enough sales to achieve low unit costs, so only publishers with a certain level of capacity could remain viable. Responsibility for text selection was transferred from the school level to selection zone committees covering a whole urban or rural area. Both appointment to the zone committees and the selection of texts were to be in general controlled by the prefectural school boards, which would recommend two or three titles per subject out of those passing screening in any particular year for the zone committees to make a final selection for the schools under their jurisdiction. The quality of education was affected in that a wider choice in accordance with local needs or preferences was prevented, while the possibility of feedback from teachers was restricted. Textbook content was also affected in that the price-fixing authority is a subsection of the Screening Research Council, so that publishers became subject to greater pressure to comply with screening comments, as well as being influenced by competition between themselves.

In the case of senior secondary textbooks, which are not free, selection after screening remained at the school level, but prices were still negotiated by another subsection of the Screening Research Council, which in this case too served to reinforce the screening process, as well as again reducing the number of viable publishers by keeping prices low. In selecting texts, teachers are also constrained by the overriding need to prepare for tertiary entrance examination, an extremely arduous hurdle in the Japanese system. Until recently, this factor particularly affected the coverage of modern history, as this field did not figure much in entrance examinations.

Immediately after the implementation of this system, textbook screening markedly toughened, provoking Ienaga's epic litigation. He was then a professor of history at the Tokyo University of Education and like many other progressive academics had taken up textbook writing as a means of contribution to the development of a society that would realize the ideals of the new Constitution. Before 1963, he had encountered some problems with screening but describes these as having been 'within a tolerable range.' Now, however, screening finally 'exceeded the limits of endurance.' (Ienaga 1995) The examiner for his textbook *New History of Japan* told him that the book was unacceptable because it was 'overall too dark.' He criticized pictures of air raid destruction and disabled veterans begging in the streets and objected to the phrases underlined in the following passage:

> The war was <u>glorified</u> as a 'sacred war' and the Japanese forces' defeats and <u>their brutal acts</u> on the battlefield were completely concealed. As a result, the majority of the Japanese people were unable to learn the truth and they were placed in a position where they had no choice but to cooperate enthusiastically in this <u>reckless war</u>.

The examiner argued that such presentation did not appropriately convey to students Japan's true situation in the maelstrom of war, but Ienaga resolved to combat this ominous trend to reactionary thought control. He resorted to litigation and challenged the screening process as an infringement of the Constitution and the Basic Education Law. He launched his first lawsuit in June 1965 in the Tokyo District Court in the form of a claim for damages against the state. He cited 130 instances of contested screening comments.

Apart from those related to the war, another concerned his statement that the myths surrounding the foundation of the Imperial House and the legends of the earliest Emperors were unhistorical and devised to establish the imperial clan's claim to supremacy (a universal phenomenon in early human history, as he realized). Another comment referred to social tensions surrounding the growing popularity of Western clothes for city women in the 1920s (the flapper era, deplored by conservatives everywhere). Numerous other points had been held likely to undermine the desirable image that students should form of their country's history.

As will be discussed later, this lawsuit continued for decades at various levels, but meanwhile, in June 1967, Ienaga instituted a second supplementary suit, also in the Tokyo District Court. This one was brought against the Education Minister, seeking the cancellation of the administrative decision, and was the first suit on which a judgment was delivered. This was the Sugimoto Judgment of July 1970 which marked virtually a complete success for Ienaga. Although the screening process itself was not declared unconstitutional, it was ruled that intervention exceeding the correction of typographical and plain factual errors and extending to the text's content contravened the spirit of the constitution, as well as the Basic Education Law. The state's role was to provide proper conditions for education, not to intervene in its content, so long as this met the essential standards of the curriculum. The judge therefore ordered the state to cancel the disqualification of the original text.

Although the Education Ministry appealed against this decision and ultimately had it reversed many years later, while right wing extremists issued their customary death threats to all involved, the Sugimoto Judgment contributed to a degree of caution in screening policy during the 1970s. Two other intermediate judgments, those of Takatsu on the first suit in 1974 and of Azegami on the second suit in 1975, were also still generally favorable to Ienaga. Other broadly favorable factors were that through most of the decade, left wing administrations were in power in most of the larger cities, which influenced the school boards, while in the latter half the LDP's hold on government was tenuous, and there was less conservative pressure on the Ministry. Variety among texts also tended to grow, as authorship broadened from academic circles to include many practicing teachers.

This phase of what one of Ienaga's lawyers called 'a golden age of Japanese justice,' combined with low profile politics, was abruptly shattered in 1980 by the 'Second "bias in textbooks" Attack,' following that of 1955. It was heralded in 1979 by an article under the title 'The New Deplorable Textbook Question,' echoing that used on an earlier occasion. The writer, Ishii Itcho, had been a main mover in the earlier attack. He had once been an executive in the Teachers' Union but was expelled in the course of factional struggles; subsequently, he was paid handsomely by the LDP for agitation against the union.

In 1980, the year that the party regained secure control of both houses in the Diet, its organ *Liberal News* ran a series of articles expanding Ishii's accusations. These had originally centered on stories appearing in National Language textbooks, which were described as fostering left wing attitudes, but soon extended to other fields, prompted not only by the LDP education policy clique but also by scholars in the Conquer Communism Alliance and financial interests. The latter, for example, opposed material on industrial pollution.

The attack on Social Studies was pursued in an adverse report by academics at the Tsukuba University. This attacked textbook coverage of demonstrations and popular activism, especially the accompanying illustrations, contenting that they inflamed student unrest and violence and argued that the only proper political role for the nation at large lies in electing politicians, to whom all political action should then be entrusted. Sales of this report were widely promoted by LDP members.

Next, in March 1981 a right wing historian Nagoshi Futaranosuke was invited to address the Upper House Budget Committee session on the faults of history texts. He particularly deplored the omission from most texts of any mention of Admiral Togo, the supreme hero of the Russo-Japanese War of 1904-05, regarded by traditionalists as an exemplary patriot comparable with Nelson in British tradition. On another occasion, Nagoshi pointed out that Togo was even commemorated by a brand of 'Togo beer' in Finland, so should not be neglected in his own country. It is true that in Finland, Japan's victory over Russia was welcomed as opening up prospects for Finland's liberation from Russian rule.

The rightward leaning Democratic Socialist Party also helped to inflame conservative resentment with the accusation that, by the system of free textbooks, the government was financing Communist propaganda in schools, as well as supporting Communist publishers. The LDP's Textbook Problem Subcommittee explored means of strengthening legal control over textbooks, and it became apparent that, under all these pressures, screening comments were shifting from the previous largely negative policy of deletions to a more pro-active policy of specifying desired revisions.

It was against this background that the media paid such close attention to the release of screened texts in June 1982, which led to the international textbook uproar described earlier. Following this, as mentioned there, the Education Minister declared that 'necessary consideration would be given to international understanding' in the treatment of history, and this instruction was entered among the screening standards prescriptions. It had little effect, however, on the new intensified screening policy, which Ienaga described as 'unprecedentedly severe in my nearly thirty years of writing.'

Considerable opposition was mobilized, however, particularly by a wide range of authors, editors, and concerned citizens organized in the Citizens' Association to Study the Textbook Question, which has since continued to function, publishing a monthly organ, *The Citizen's Voice.* Another protest group was the Social Studies Textbook Authors' Forum, which held yearly meetings to publicize current experience with screening. Ienaga also instituted a third lawsuit, though the first two were still being appealed. The occasion of this was his latest textbook, *New History of Japan B,* screened in 1980 and 1983, when he objected to eight screening comments. The book was eventually authorized by his compromising on the six mandatory 'corrections' and ignoring the two 'suggested improvements,' despite informal pressure, as he was legally able to do. But at the beginning of 1984, he launched the third suit, again claiming damages from the state, as well as the restoration of the original text. The details of this litigation will be described in the next chapter, using the screening comments to illustrate the Council's procedure. Ienaga's support group, the National League for Support of the School Textbook Screening Suit, remained another strong focus of protest.

From this time, however, the judgments delivered in his various suits became unfavorable, apparently reflecting the reactionary trends under Prime Minister Nakasone. The recommendations of Nakasone's Provisional Education Council, which favored both greater diversity in education and stronger controls, led to a major recasting in 1989 of both Course Guidelines and the screening procedure. In the lead-up to this revision, the Diet Members' League for the Study of Textbooks particularly agitated for the inclusion of Admiral Togo as a prescribed topic in history texts. Education Ministry bureaucrats were generally favorable but meanwhile the Nakasone cabinet was replaced, and the new Education Minister happened to be of antimilitaristic leanings and blocked these maneuvers when they were exposed by the *Asahi*.

After the next cabinet reorganization, however, a compromise was reached whereby Togo was included among 42 historical characters spanning the whole of Japanese history, who were recommended as suitable for inclusion in courses. None was compulsory, but it turned out that Togo was included in all primary texts subsequently published, apparently another sign of the decline of left wing and pacifistic influence in education and the concomitant revival of conservative values.

The most significant feature of the 1989 Course Guidelines from the standpoint of teaching about the war was the division of the secondary level Social Studies curriculum to separate the history and geography component from civics, which included politics and economics. This division facilitated an easing of restrictions on history while tightening controls on current political and social areas, where the official line is more strictly pursued than ever.

The relaxation on history, contrary to Nakasone's original design, had become inevitable through a steady accumulation of factors during the 1980s. These included the 1982 textbook uproar, with the resulting policy decision on 'international understanding;' Ienaga's campaign; repeated apologies for the war by political leaders, including the new Emperor; more widely available research and information on the war; and above all the need for frankness to secure trust in the Asia-Pacific region for Japan's expanded diplomatic and quasi-military Peace Keeping Operations roles. Later contributing factors, as mentioned earlier, were the fall of the LDP and the consequent weakening of the Diet members' education clique, as well as greater resulting independence for the school boards.

On the other hand, control over civics and other areas was intensified by the introduction of a more burdensome screening procedure. In the earlier system, most texts after initial screening were accorded 'conditional qualification,' subject to specified requirements, with some scope for negotiation and without a tight schedule. In the new system, however, after initial screening, except where texts qualify at once, screening comments are issued in the form of a 'table of points for attention,' and the decision is reserved without any commitment as to final qualification. Authors or publishers are allowed only 42 days to submit a 'table of amendments.' After this is examined, a second 'table of amendments' may be required, again with a deadline of 42 days. In view of the costs incurred, with no assurance of qualification until the end of the process, authors and publishers are under still greater pressure than in the past to acquiesce in screening policy lines.

Areas where debate has been suppressed are the legality of the Self Defense Forces, the degree of respect due to the Emperor system, the use of the national flag, Japanese 'economic aggression' in developing countries, environmental issues, U.S. Middle Eastern policy, and the essential character of Japanese foreign policy as based on the U.S. Security Treaty within the United Nations framework. Critics of screening policy particularly condemn these latter aspects as suppressing any questioning of the real nature of the United Nations, describing it as actually a puppet show run by the United States as the 'world *kempei*.' In 1993, a new round of litigation against the new screening system was launched in the Yokohama District Court, distinct from Ienaga's but intended to inherit his crusade in the new context. The issues raised will be sketched in the next chapter.

The new screening system could of course also be used to restrict coverage of the war as in the past but, for the reasons noted, 'self-regulation' is allowed in this area. After some years experience of the new system, Ienaga has admitted to some surprise at the degree to which Japan's responsibility for inflicting harm through the war has been covered in new edition history texts. His own history text, subject of the third lawsuit, has been reissued with the disputed points restored, without any impediment from screening, though this did not mean that the question of the constitutionality of screening was settled.

At all events, the term 'aggression,' described as the 'sorest point of dispute' in the controversy of the 1980s, was given a 'free pass' in the new guidelines. A case is quoted where its use has even been promoted in a screening comment to the effect: 'should this not be expressed in such a way that the nature of "aggression" is more clearly understood?' Positive terminology in contrast to the earlier 'neutral terms' or euphemism is encouraged. Frank coverage has been allowed of such topics as comfort women; war compensation; colonialism; the Nanking Massacre, allowing figures up to 160,000 for the number of victims, although sources are usually demanded for figures; Unit 731; the 'three lightnings' search and destroy campaign in North China; forced labor; the exploitation rather than liberation of Southeast Asia; the Emperor's wartime role, degree of responsibility and exemption from prosecution for 'the smooth conduct of occupation policy;' and the battle of Okinawa. One restriction has been the deletion of rape as unsuitable for junior pupils. The term 'Asia-Pacific War' is the preferred standard term.

Although political fluidity reduced Diet pressures on Ministry policy, right wing resistance remains persistent in various contexts. A couple of attempts to annul qualification of certain texts after they passed screening were undertaken by legal action in 1984 and 1991 without success, but pressure on textbook publishers has had some effect. From July 1993 to February 1994, a series of media articles attacked texts mentioning comfort women and more particularly the description of the Nanking massacre in a senior secondary World History text which had reached the stage of approved sample copy. The publisher was approached repeatedly with demands to produce evidence for statements made, for example, about orders to 'requisition' supplies locally. The issue was taken up by some politicians with right wing links who, through the Education Ministry, pressed for revisions before the textbook was distributed to selection committees. The book's producers accordingly made revisions, such as an implication that plunder arose from individual initiative under hardship rather than official policy but also counter-balanced this by inserting a new passage on orders to take no prisoners. This addition was allowed to stand but was attacked by the *Sankei* and in other quarters, who produced a diary source indicating that some thousands of captured prisoners had been put to work in Shanghai. This attack in turn affected the screening of a text in Japanese History in toning down the treatment of this point.

Later in 1994, an association of ex-servicemen and Self Defense Force members called the League of Compatriots sent an elaborate facsimile transmission to the publishers of a junior secondary level text demanding that it portray the Imperial House as the pivot of national integration, treat the founding myths as embodying the national ethos, recognize the nation's heroes, and cultivate a national defense spirit. It attacked the common tendency of textbooks now to promote class struggle and the Tokyo Trial view of history.

At the same time, an avowedly nationalistic textbook was produced as a successor to the earlier *New History of Japan,* sponsored by Prime Minister Nakasone but poorly produced, attacked from abroad, and of limited success at home. Its compilers, who had belonged to the National Congress to Safeguard Japan, now brought out as its replacement the *Latest History of Japan.* Apart from its submission for screening as a textbook, it was promoted for a more general readership, notably by a leaflet sold at Shinto shrines and widely distributed. It was claimed to be inspired by a 'love of our history' and to counter the 'masochistic, condemnatory bias' of other texts, to show proper honor for the Imperial House, objectively describe the Greater East Asia War, and expose the unfairness of the Tokyo Trials. The screening process, however, imposed some revisions. The statement that 'the aim of the Greater East Asia War was self-preservation and the construction of the Greater East Asia Co-prosperity Sphere' was revised to 'the aim of the war was represented to be' such. A description of Manchukuo as aiming at cooperative construction by its component races was deleted. Screening comments also strengthened wording on the Nanking massacre and introduced an account of forced labor and exploitation in the colonies and occupied areas. The authors, however, persisted in refusing to include the Emperor's disclaimer of divinity.

As screening in this case was used to curb nationalistic excesses, some critics of the system concede that it may have merit on this score, which paradoxically was its original aim under the early occupation. Such considerations have led the complainant in the Yokohama lawsuit to take a cautious approach to the question of the abolition of screening. It is noted that the *Latest History* was rather more widely selected in its first year than Ienaga's revised text.

A personal communication from an activist teacher in contact with Yumi Lee represents the main problem for education about the war as now not being a matter of political concern or remissness but technical. As history texts cover the whole of Japanese history they cannot be treated adequately in school hours, so some students only reach modern history in the ubiquitous cram school (a privately run supplement to public education). It is true that more questions on modern history now appear in university entrance examinations and senior high schools attempt to cater for this but tend to be forced into a partial choice between Japanese and world history. In the technical stream Japanese history does not figure in entrance examinations. Consequently, many students miss detailed treatment of the war. The informant favors greater emphasis on modern history and an approach designed to promote active discussion of it.

7 Ienaga and the course of textbook litigation

Ienaga Saburo was born in 1913 and received his early schooling during Japan's era of liberalism and conciliatory diplomacy, which may have left him with some subliminal leaning to such values—so much in contrast with the succeeding period of reaction. The same probably applied to many of his contemporaries, which would help to explain the durability of the new Constitution—something that even its framers could not confidently predict.

Although his National History lessons began as usual with the Shinto creation and national foundation myths, he also recalls reading an extracurricular history book that began with the Stone Age, causing him to reflect that this did not agree with Shinto creationism. The study of evolution does not appear to have been suppressed in the context of strictly biological studies, unlike the case of some southern states in the United States, and the Emperor himself, who was a competent marine biologist, kept a bust of Darwin in his library. But when such things were imported into the historical field, there was trouble. A celebrated trial in the late 1930s, when reaction was rampant, concerned a general critical analysis of early myths and legends by Professor Tsuda Sokichi of Waseda University. He was convicted of infringement of the publications law on the grounds of disrespect to the Imperial House and sentenced to three months imprisonment, though this was suspended.

When Ienaga began his tertiary courses in 1934, the universities, which until shortly before had been hotbeds of liberal and Marxist thought, had become politically quiescent. The main factors in this were the nationalistic fervor stirred up by the Manchurian incident and the successful brainwashing of leading radicals by the Thought Police. The resulting public recantations by these brought widespread disillusionment among their erstwhile following.

Ienaga began teaching history at senior secondary level a few months before Pearl Harbor. He was, of course, required to teach the highly nationalistic content of the curriculum and was well aware of the possibility that any hint of departure from orthodoxy could well be reported to the Thought Police or Kempeitai, even by his students. He describes himself as having, like many

109

others, taken refuge in 'academic detachment'—a course which in retrospect he felt dishonorable.

Freedom to teach or write as he chose came abruptly in 1945 when the previous taboos were lifted—a change that he welcomed with enthusiasm. Soon afterwards he produced a *New History of Japan* for public sale, freely expressing his interpretation of Japanese history, with its climax in the new Constitution guaranteeing popular sovereignty and human rights. Although he welcomed the dissolution of the armed forces, he did not particularly deal with the pacifistic aspect of the Constitution, and he later regarded this omission as a sign of complacency. He seems to have regarded the defeat as conclusively eliminating any danger of future militaristic reaction.

His writing, however, was successful enough to induce publishers, expecting continued freedom in the publishing field, to commission him to write history texts, which he began to do in 1952. In these he treated the founding myths as such and instead of traditional emphasis on emperors and public figures concentrated on the development of the nation as a whole—those who, as he put it, were the 'people who sustain history.' He saw this approach as promoting the ideals of the new Constitution, though it was later questioned as betraying a Marxist type of bias.

For a number of years, he had no material trouble with screening, and there was no pressure to present the Asia-Pacific War as in any way justifiable or excusable. But as the Cold War and 'reverse course' intensified, with a rapidity beyond all expectations, he came to realize that he had been overconfident and only fully appreciated the Constitution as he saw it being undermined by creeping rearmament and stricter controls on education. Finally, as related earlier, he experienced such severe screening in 1963 on such issues as the treatment of myths, social history, and the war that he felt his only alternatives to be either to cease writing or to challenge the screening system itself. To give up would be merely a repetition of his wartime inertia, so he chose to challenge the system.

He began by having opposition Diet members question the screening process in the course of debates, but within the existing balance of power, no satisfactory replies could be obtained. He therefore decided to resort to legal action by way of challenging the constitutionality of screening, since at least a court would have to frame a reasoned ruling on his complaint. He had already played some part in litigation on educational issues, having appeared as a witness in two lawsuits brought by teachers. Both of these had opposed other measures designed by the Education Ministry to strengthen controls, parallel to the screening of textbooks.

The first arose from a system of teacher Duty Ratings introduced from 1957 which had the effect of transforming school principals, who had earlier tended to belong to the Teachers' Union, into agents of Education Ministry control. The second measure was a nationally uniform system of Achievement Tests for junior secondary pupils introduced in 1961. Some teachers who had opposed this as too mechanical and restrictive had been disciplined and sued the Ministry. This case continued for many years and later interacted with Ienaga's own lawsuits.

In both cases Ienaga had testified for academic freedom and formed contact with lawyers sympathetic to the cause. Three of them now agreed to act for him in his projected lawsuit 'within his economic circumstances,' which solved the problem of the massive costs that might have been expected. The other initial problem was to obtain the agreement of his publishers, Sanseido, who would need to testify on some steps in the screening process, but they agreed to allow staff to testify as to facts.

Ienaga felt no assurance of success but felt that the attempt itself was significant for mobilizing resistance to a revival of the prewar misuse of education, which had led to a loss of autonomous judgment among the people and prevented any effective resistance to the war. As he expressed it:

> I hoped that my advocacy through the court struggle might make even one more person realize the importance of this issue and provide a breakthrough to the abolition of the screening system which aims to control the nation's thought through textbooks, or at least a radical reform of its present mode of operation.

His marathon campaign, which he later described as having become 'his reason to live,' certainly had an impact on public opinion, as already noted, and contributed to the ultimate relaxation of restriction on textbook coverage of the war. It is also claimed to have had the effect of inhibiting the Ministry from introducing even more severe measures. Critics in the Ministry have described him as unsuited to be a textbook author, partly because he was too specialized in ideological history and partly because of his critical style. The right wing have either threatened him and his supporters with violence or disparaged him as one of the academics who had obtained appointment only through the occupation period purge of others who were abler and more patriotic.

His support group, however, called the National League for Support of the School Textbook Screening Suit, grew from some initial thousands to well over 20,000 and has throughout issued a monthly *Textbook Suit News,* as well as publishing multivolume transcripts of court proceedings. Apart from formal membership, there has been considerable informal encouragement and financial aid, with the result that Ienaga's legal team has expanded to 30 members. The movement is also described as unique in that it is free from the factionalism and splits common among large popular movements, particularly in Japan, where this feature is also conspicuous in political parties. The crusade also came to attract widespread international interest and support. The *Times* described it as 'a litmus test for assessing Japan's thinking on its military future and remorse for the Imperial Forces' atrocities.' In South Korea, a million

111

signatures were collected in its support and the 1995 conference for the Japanese Studies Association of Australia adopted a resolution to this effect.

In Ienaga's opening address to his first lawsuit, he described his motives:

> As one Japanese who passed through these tragic experiences, I cannot overlook in silence the reality of the present screening system, which has trampled the Constitution and the Basic Education Law in an attempt to pluck the spirit of pacifism and democracy from the nation's consciousness. My aim as plaintiff in this lawsuit is comprised in a single point namely that, by the fair judgment of this court, the present screening system be declared an illegal exercise of power exceeding the proper scope of educational administration.

On a more personal note also: 'I feel deeply guilty for having been a passive witness to my country's ruin.... I am just a humble citizen now but, even if I cannot achieve much, I wish to atone for my fault in not offering resistance earlier.'

Hearings in this lawsuit, claiming damages against the state, began in June 1965 in the Tokyo District Court and followed the usual pattern of Japanese court proceedings, referred to as the 'continental system,' in which sessions are held at intervals of weeks or perhaps months, each devoted to testimony by one or two witnesses. Ienaga's witnesses included a wide range of academics, teachers, and publishing employees who either tackled the legality of the screening system, addressed questions of educational theory and practice, or gave expert testimony on the accuracy of points raised in screening comments. Education Ministry witnesses countered with arguments both to the effect that children's lack of maturity requires guidance rather than reliance on their own initiative and that it cannot be left to teachers to ensure nationwide uniformity of standards and equal opportunity in education. The only means of achieving this was to base instruction on textbooks screened to accord with a nationally standardized curriculum. 'The state is the sole agency for focusing the multidimensional demands of the nation as a whole.' (Fujiwara 1988)

As mentioned earlier, Ienaga instituted a second lawsuit, this time against the Ministry seeking the cancellation of its administrative decision, in June 1967. This was the first to reach a judgment, that by Judge Sugimoto in July 1970, which was completely favorable to Ienaga. Among his reasons, the judge stated that: 'The state is to be neutral in regard to the person's inner values and is not to intrude on the individual's inner life by way of imposing value judgments.' He viewed the child's right to education as part of the 'right to maintain the minimum standards of wholesome and cultured living' as expressed in Article 25 of the Constitution.

> The Constitution's guarantee of the right of the nation, in particular children, to receive education implies that a democratic state presup-

poses the existence of citizens each possessing autonomous conscious-ness.... As the teacher's role is to enable pupils to receive information and to stimulate in them reflectiveness and creativity, it is indispensable that academic freedom be guaranteed to teachers. (Fujiwara 1988)

He accordingly ordered that the disqualification of Ienaga's textbook be canceled.

Although it was noted in later years that Judge Sugimoto had never again been appointed to a metropolitan court, suggesting retaliation by the estab-lishment, his judgment influenced some others in succeeding years. The Min-istry appealed meanwhile to the Tokyo High Court while the first lawsuit continued in the District Court. The latter in July 1974 delivered the Takatsu judgment which still represented a partial success for Ienaga. Although this judgment placed more emphasis on the public character of education and more clearly accepted the constitutionality of screening, it awarded Ienaga ¥100,000 in damages for excesses and impropriety in some of the screening comments.

For example, Judge Takatsu ruled that the 'recklessness' of the war was accepted nationally as common sense. Ienaga, however, questioned the judge's expertise in ruling on points of historical accuracy, as well as his con-centration on this aspect at the expense of the question of legality, so he ap-pealed to the Tokyo High Court. The state also appealed with the aim of re-versing the unfavorable aspects of the judgment.

The next judgment to be delivered was that by Judge Azegami in the High Court in December 1975 on the second lawsuit. This was also favorable to Ienaga in dismissing the Ministry's appeal against the Sugimoto judgment. Although screening again was not ruled unconstitutional, the screening com-ments at issue were ruled illegal under the Basic Education Law as constitut-ing an 'abuse of administrative discretion.' The Ministry, however, appealed to the Supreme Court.

The next partly related development was a Supreme Court judgment in May 1976 on the school Achievement Test suit which, in relation to such tests, set strict limits on state control over education and clearly reflected the principles of the Sugimoto judgment. It was ruled that state intervention must be 'as restrained as possible within a necessary and appropriate scope.' Con-trol was not to impede children's growth as free and independent individuals, as education was essentially a cultural process relating to inner values, not to be subject to fluctuating political pressures or to the prewar pattern of formal-ism and uniformity.

Subsequent judgments, however, showed a consistent trend to reaction against this 'golden age,' following the 'Second "bias in education" Attack' in 1980. In April 1982 in the Supreme Court, the Nakamura judgment on the second lawsuit annulled the Azegami judgment and remanded the suit to the High Court. The reason was that the Ministry had raised a new argument against Ienaga to the effect that there could be no 'benefit from litigation' because course guidelines had changed, and the qualification of the original text, even if ordered by the court, would serve no useful purpose. So Judge Naka-mura referred the argument to the High Court as the appropriate level to rule on it. Ienaga reacted to this by appending to this suit also a claim for damages by the state. This in turn was referred to the District Court and action followed on both levels until 1989 when, after an unfavorable ruling in the High Court to the effect that there was no 'benefit' to Ienaga, he abandoned this second suit.

Meanwhile, at the beginning of 1984, Ienaga had responded to the tough-ened screenings of 1980 and 1983 by instituting his third lawsuit in the Dis-trict Court for damages from the state and the restoration of his original text. The details of the disputed points provide a useful illustration of the screening process. Ienaga had compromised by revisions to passages subject to the man-datory 'correction' comments and ignored the nonmandatory 'improvements,' though in the lawsuit he objected to the improper pressures encountered even in the latter cases. The first four points refer to the 1980 screening and the oth-ers to 1983.

1. Original MS: [footnote] Immediately after the occupation of Nanking the Japanese army slaughtered numerous Chinese soldiers and civilians. This is known as the Nanking *Atrocity* [transliterated from English].

Correction comment: This could be construed to mean that the army organized a massacre immediately after the occupation, so revise the expression so that it is not interpreted in this way. Be sure to state that it was an incident occurring 'during the disorder.'

Account as qualified: In the heat of battling the fierce resistance of the Chinese forces, the Japanese army occupied Nanking and slaugh-tered ... (as earlier).

2. Original MS: Honen and Shinran [medieval Buddhist reformers with many modern adherents] were suppressed by the Court, but Shin-ran boldly protested and refused to submit.

Improvement comment: Shinran criticized the Court in his later reminiscences, so this account is inappropriate, as it could be construed to mean that he criticized it at the time of suppression.

Qualified unaltered.

3. Original MS: [In the course of the Court's campaign to suppress the shogunate in the Imperial Restoration over 1867-68] The Court's forces sought popular support by proclaiming such policies as halving the land tax, so volunteer militia willingly joined in the expedition against the Shogunate, but later the Court executed members of the mi-litia as a 'spurious court army' and did not halve the tax.

Correction comment: The Court did not make such a promise as halving the land tax. Reconsider the part treating the 'Court's forces' as issuing this policy.

Account as qualified: Popular voluntary militia also joined the forces for suppressing the shogunate. Some of these militia sought popular support by erecting public notices of a policy to halve the then land tax of the former shogunate. But in the course of their advance the Court executed some of this group as a 'spurious court army.' The land tax was not halved and the peasants who had entertained hopes in the emergence of a new government realized that these would not necessarily be realized.

[Although this revision looks like an admission of error by Ienaga, it was established in court that his account reflected the consensus of historians and the 'correction' was an imposition of the examiner's private view. Actually, this and the preceding point had been thought disrespectful to the Imperial House.]

4. Original MS: In China, with the Hsian Incident as a turning point [the arrest of Chiang Kai-shek by mutinous troops refusing to fight the Communists instead of Japan] the Nationalist Government and the Communist Party formed a united front against Japan and adopted a firm stance to resist Japanese aggression and restore Chinese sovereignty [against colonialism generally].

Improvement comment: In education it is not desirable to use terms with a negative value judgment regarding the actions' of one's own country. These should be unified by objective expressions such as 'military advance.'

Qualified unaltered.

[Thus even in 1980, contrary to the impression triggering the 1982 international uproar, the word 'aggression' was not actually banned.]

5. Original MS: [footnote] a. When the Japanese army occupied Nanking, they slaughtered large numbers of Chinese troops and civilians and many Japanese officers and men violated Chinese women. This is known as the Nanking massacre. b. [In guerrilla warfare] The Japanese army everywhere murdered inhabitants, burned out villages and violated women, inflicting immense harm to the lives, property and chastity of the Chinese.

Correction comment: Delete references to 'violating women' and 'chastity.' The phenomenon of assault on women by troops is something that occurs commonly throughout the world, so to refer to this in relation to the Japanese army alone is unsuitable in terms of selectivity and sequence, as well as overemphasizing particular incidents.

Account as qualified: a. When the Japanese army ... (as earlier) ... officers and men committed such acts as assault and pillage ... Nanking Massacre.

b. 'Violated women' and 'chastity' deleted.

6. Original MS: [footnote] A Unit called 731 was established on the outskirts of Harbin and for many years until the Soviet Union entered the war continued such atrocities as capturing, experimenting on, vivisecting, and killing several thousand foreign nationals, mainly Chinese.

Correction comment: At the present time no reliable scholarly research, articles or books have been published on Unit 731, so it is premature to take up this matter in a textbook. The whole is ordered deleted.

Qualified after deletion.

7. Original MS: The Sino-Japanese War began in 1894. In fighting extending to the following year, the Japanese army was consistently victorious but in Korea, which became the battleground, popular resistance to Japan repeatedly occurred.

Correction comment: It is not clear what is meant by resistance to Japan. Delete from 'in Korea.'

Account as qualified: In 1894 the Sino-Japanese war finally began and in fighting extending to the following year the Japanese army was repeatedly victorious but in Korea, which became the battleground, often failed to obtain popular cooperation in such matters as labor and requisitioning materials.

8. Original MS: [footnote] Okinawa Prefecture became a theater of land combat and approximately 160,000 residents, old and young, male and female, met untimely deaths amid the conflict. More than a few of these were killed by the Japanese army.

Correction comment: As mass suicides were the most numerous among the people of Okinawa Prefecture who fell victim, the whole aspect of the battle of Okinawa is not clear without adding an account of mass suicides.

Account as qualified: Okinawa Prefecture became ... (as earlier) ... met untimely deaths by shelling, bombing, or being driven to mass suicide. More than a few were killed by the Japanese army.

While this lawsuit was proceeding, including a visit to Okinawa, the Suzuki judgment on the first lawsuit was delivered in the High Court in March 1986. It followed the new unfavorable pattern by overturning the Takatsu judgment. Without consideration of any of the points at issue, it was ruled that the screening process was constitutional and legal and that comments 'with appropriate basis' were acceptable. As there was no attempt to define such a basis, the Ministry's discretion became in effect completely unrestricted. The reasoning was:

Textbooks are a special class of book used in school education for children or pupils undeveloped mentally and physically, so that certain

standards must be maintained in their content, their use being compulsory and suited to the powers of comprehension appropriate to the level of development, requiring an organization and sequence corresponding to the structure of each curriculum. (Fujiwara 1988)

As this judgment could be seen as conflicting with the flexibility in personal development and limitations to state intervention implied in the Supreme Court's Achievement Test judgment of 1976, Ienaga appealed to that court.

The first judgment on the third lawsuit was issued as the Kato judgment in the District Court in October 1989. This marked Ienaga's first though limited success since 1975, as he was awarded ¥100,000 damages for the unjustified comment on the volunteer militia in the Imperial Restoration. But the other comments were not ruled improper. Regarding Unit 731, for example, the court accepted the view of the conservative historian Hata Ikuhiko to the effect that its inclusion in textbooks would have been premature because the material then available (such as *The Devil's Gluttony*) was merely oral history which is less reliable than documentary history. Ienaga ridiculed such a rigid distinction, particularly as Hata now accepted the validity of the Norbert Fell Report, which was entirely based on oral testimony!

Regarding the deletion of mention of rape in China, Judge Kato conceded that it was difficult to agree with the deletion of rape only, while allowing murder and arson to stand, but maintained that it did not entirely lack a rational basis in terms of current social attitudes. Ienaga appealed to the High Court. Although he hoped that the publicity surrounding the third lawsuit would favorably influence the Supreme Court on the first suit, such expectations were abruptly dashed by the Kabe judgment of March 1993, dismissing his appeal. It was issued quite abruptly without any notice to Ienaga or his counsel, and he first learned of it from press reporters. Its content was also brief and peremptory, again failing to consider specific points. Although it quoted as a precedent the Supreme Court Judgment on the Achievement Test suit, to the effect that state intervention in education must be 'as restrained as possible within a necessary and appropriate scope,' it ignored the strict conditions implied in that judgment and applied it in a reverse direction. It was ruled that the screening process had remained within 'rational and necessary limitations with regard to public welfare' and was therefore constitutional and legal.

Although there was no further avenue of appeal on this suit, the third suit brought a further success for Ienaga a few months later, in October in the Kawakami judgment in the High Court. This awarded him a further ¥200,000 damages for illegality in two more screening comments, namely the deletion of rape in guerrilla war and the toning down of the description of the Nanking Massacre. As the Ministry did not appeal these points or the earlier point on the Restoration militia, these are regarded as a definite success for Ienaga. But

117

as the screening process had not been declared unconstitutional, he appealed to the Supreme Court, where it remained at the time of writing.

Although, in view of the Supreme Court's record on the previous lawsuits, a finding of unconstitutionality is quite unlikely, Ienaga's epic crusade may be credited with having achieved the beneficial side effects already noted. He himself has been philosophical, saying from the perspective of a true historian that 'there is no other way to live than to do the best one can, always within the given historical conditions.'

Besides, his crusade does not end with him. He has found a noteworthy successor, whose initiation of a comparable lawsuit in the Yokohama District Court forms a suitable postscript to Ienaga's efforts. The plaintiff is Takashima Nobuyoshi, a senior secondary level teacher and visiting lecturer at Meiji University. His motive, as already mentioned, is to challenge afresh the screening system as revised since 1989, which presents rather different problems than those arising in Ienaga's time.

Takashima had already experienced six screenings of his textbook before he decided to rebel at the seventh and launched his suit at his local district court in 1993. The case at issue was his contribution to a textbook in the field Contemporary Society, a subject introduced by the Education Ministry with the stated aim of allowing more debate and more liberal screening but which tended to exceed the intended scope.

1. Under the topic 'We and the Contemporary Media' he had taken as an example of overreporting the intensive coverage of the Emperor's death which was regarded by the Ministry as an unsuitable example. In its view, it was necessary to explain the media policy of 'framing programs with a sentiment of mourning befitting the symbol of the nation.'

2. Under the same topic, he had taken the following examples of manipulation of the press for political purposes:

> In the 1991 Gulf War not only Iraq but the multinational force centered on the United States maintained thorough control of news. The multinational force arranged for the media to report that the counterattack on Kuwaiti territory would begin with a landing from the sea but actually the attack was made from the land. The command is said to have thanked journalists, saying: 'Owing to you, the enemy counterattack was feeble.'

It was also reported that Hussein had used poison gas to suppress the domestic Kurdish revolt, but the U.S. government already knew that this was not a fact. It had been established in analysis by U.S. army laboratories that the gas used on the Kurds was not Iraqi but that held by neighboring countries.

Screening disallowed these passages on the grounds that the later reports they were based on were untrustworthy, although this could only reinforce the intended warning against too great trust in the media.

3. In his teaching experience, Takashima realized that senior students were already well aware of the facts of Japan's aggression but wished to learn more about its underlying causes. This involved both official colonialism and individual soldiers' contempt for Asians, of which he had heard a great deal in war research in Southeast Asia. There was also the question of Japan's abrupt change from premodern respect for continental culture. So under the topic 'Japan in Asia,' he combined these themes in a study of Fukuzawa Yukichi's 1885 article *Abandoning Asia and Joining Europe* advocating primacy to Westernization with the corollary that 'Asian countries were to be treated (i.e., colonized) in the same way as by Westernizers.'

Screening demanded rewriting on the grounds that Fukuzawa could be construed as advocating a 'Western-style heavy-handed approach to Korea—a one-sided interpretation.' But no agreement could be reached on a revision.

4. Under the same topic he had also written:

> Mine sweepers of the Sea Self-Defense Forces were urgently dispatched to remove mines laid in the Persian Gulf during the Gulf War. Many voices were raised in Southeast Asian countries to the effect that they would have wished to be consulted before this dispatch was decided upon.
>
> Screening comment: The mine sweepers were dispatched for the safety of Japanese tankers, and there was no need to consult Southeast Asian countries. Is this not excessively subservient?

The passage was ordered deleted—an action which in itself is a symptom of the persistence of the Fukuzawa syndrome, at least as usually interpreted.

Takashima also acquired an effective support group. His purpose, unlike Ienaga's, was not the immediate abolition of textbook control because from his current teaching experience he was aware of other dangers. He rather favored phasing it out through an interim independent agency, broadly based and with less binding and more transparent proceedings.

Table 7.1
Chronology of Textbook Litigation
(judgments are indicated by the presiding judges' names)

	1st Lawsuit	2nd Lawsuit	3rd Lawsuit
June 1965	Began in Tokyo District Court		
June 1967		Began in Tokyo District Court	
July 1970		Sugimoto (Appealed to Tokyo High Court)	

	1st Lawsuit	2nd Lawsuit	3rd Lawsuit
July 1974	Takatsu (Appealed Tokyo High Court)		
December 1975		Azegami (Appealed to Supreme Court)	
(May 1976	Supreme Court Achievement Test Suit Judgment)		
April 1982		Nakamura (Remanded to High Court then to District Court and back to High Court)	
January 1984		Began in Tokyo District Court	
March 1986	Suzuki (Appealed to Supreme Court)		
July 1989		Abandoned	
October 1989			Kato (Appealed to Tokyo High Court)
March 1993	Kabe (concluded)		
(1993	Yokohama Lawsuit began)		
October 1993			Kawakami (Appealed to Supreme Court) (pending)

8 Right wing revisionist counter-attacks

As related earlier, the spread in recent years of neonationalist revisionist arguments on the war, with increased plausibility and sophistication, has repeatedly emboldened public figures (as well as others) to make rash statements about the war and Japanese colonialism, usually leading to their dismissal from public office. The most conspicuous exception to this fate has been Hashimoto Ryutaro, head of the War Bereaved Families Association, who became prime minister early in 1996 and successfully weathered a Lower House election in October.

The authors of such literature, as noted, cover a fairly wide range of articulate 'nationalist intellectuals' but virtually no professional historians. This itself need not be conclusive, as gifted amateurs may sometimes contribute a perspective missed by professionals too constrained by the orthodoxies of their discipline, but the nationalist revisionists in Japan are at least as bound by predilections as any group, as will be seen in an outline of their approach. Some points they raise may occasionally be worth considering, as the study of the Asia-Pacific War has been so saturated on all sides by ideological bias, propaganda, and national interests that an objective consensus has been more difficult to achieve than, for example, in the case of the European phase of the Second World War. For one thing the languages of European historical sources are much more widely current than those of Asia-Pacific sources, while again the war covered by the latter involved a far greater range of contrasting cultures than the European theater. In any case, irrespective of any possible validity in revisionist arguments, our concern here is with their influence on Japanese perceptions. Readership has been considerable, going by sales, and is described by an informant as probably mainly consisting of older age groups or business or other circles supporting both the LDP and the NFP.

A source recommended as containing a representative coverage of revisionist arguments is *Showa History under Seal*, which is based on a dialogue in a symposium setting by two academics, both quite highly qualified in their fields. The title implied that the true history of the last Emperor's reign has

121

been kept 'under seal' for ulterior motives by the allies and the collaborationist Japanese establishment. The leading discussant is Komuro Naoki, holder of a Doctorate of Law from Tokyo University, who has also studied at the Massachusetts Institute of Technology, Michigan, and Harvard. His books include The *Collapse of the Soviet Empire* (1980 and regarded as prophetic), *The Tragedy of South Korea,* and, as co-author, *This is how the Pacific War could have been won.* The second discussant is Watanabe Shoichi, Professor of English Literature at Sophia University, Tokyo, where he graduated, as well as studying at Munster and Oxford. His works include *Method of Intellectual Life, The Sun* [i.e. Japan] *also Rises,* and *Thus Showa History is Resurrected.* He was also co-author with Ishihara Shintaro, the prominent 'Nanking massacre denier,' of the successful *Japan That Can Say No.*

Showa History under Seal has the subtitle 'The end of masochism—50 Years after the War' and was basically a reaction to the Diet's resolution of that date. It is described as aiming to rescue Japan from the demoralization fostered by the 'Tokyo Trial view of History,' which is held to imply that the Japanese as a whole are a criminal nation. This 'polluted Showa history' has brought a loss of all national pride and pervaded society with a mood of anomie. This had been intensified by the subservience of leaders in the face of foreign accusations, notably Prime Minister Hosokawa's admission of aggression and the Diet resolution. The loss of social standards had fostered political and financial corruption, bullying in schools and the rise of aberrant cults like Aum Supreme Truth with its sarin gas attack on the Tokyo subway and the accumulation of weapons for its Armageddon. 'Since Japanese had been convinced they were a criminal race, it was felt to be a natural course for them to follow.' Although foreigners had been startled by Japan's loss of its place as 'the safest country in the world,' this was the logical outcome of the masochistic education instilled in its youth by officially approved textbooks.

Such an education system had been systematically imposed on Japan by occupation policy to promote a loss of national morale, because Ruth Benedict's well-known wartime study of Japanese society, *The Chrysanthemum and the Sword,* had attributed the intense Japanese spirit of sacrifice to Emperor-centered nationalism. This, therefore, had to be undermined by a program of 'brainwashing' before the Chinese invented the term to describe it. The speakers hoped to reverse this process by a revisionist analysis of the main accusations directed against Japan, and they defend their qualification to do so, though not professional historians, by describing 'official historians' as not being trained to evaluate data objectively but to distort it for preconceived ends. Much better, they claim, is some work by amateurs who have pursued issues more conscientiously.

Four recommended examples are: *Overview of the Nanking Incident* (1987) by Tanaka Masaaki, *Oral Records on the Nanking Incident* (1987) by Ara Ken'ichi, *The Truth of the Battle for Nanking* (1994) by Maekawa Saburo, and *This is how the Nanking Massacre was Fabricated* (1995) by Fuji Nobuo.

Nanking massacre denial

These works are singled out because the Nanking Massacre is regarded as the central symbolic theme in the 'brainwashing' of Japanese to convince them of their war guilt. The speakers, like many in the right wing, do not by any means spare the wartime leadership from criticism and in this case concede that the neglect of proper planning for supply was a factor in the course of events at Nanking. This is admitted to have been 'Japan's fatal weakness throughout the Second World War,' leading to a strategy of staking all on a reckless advance and relying on local requisitioning. Nevertheless it is asserted that such requisitioning was not contrary to international law.

Nor, to go further, did most of the deaths arising from the Nanking campaign infringe international law or usage since they consisted either of battle deaths, the shooting of prisoners attempting to escape, or the execution of plain clothes militia or guerrillas. This last category in particular is described as lacking any status under international law such as the Hague Convention, which specifies that, to qualify for the treatment prescribed for regular prisoners of war, four conditions must be fulfilled: soldiers must be in uniform, must be organized under a regular command structure, must bear visible arms, and must follow accepted usages of war. Otherwise they may be executed as outlaws or bandits, as is customary also in the case of spies. It is also permitted to investigate or arrest civilians suspected of being agents. In the nature of the campaign, as later in expanded guerrilla warfare, attacks could come from any quarter and the forces were entitled to guard against this possibility. The Americans only experienced this reality in Vietnam, long after the Tokyo Trials had condemned Japan for actions later found to be unavoidable in that form of warfare.

Even the captured regular troops, however, were not protected by international law, since to qualify as regular prisoners of war it is necessary to be included in an organized surrender under a regular command. This was not the case in Nanking, where the command fled after ordering the troops to fight to the death, so that the proper conditions were not fulfilled. Individual surrenders may be handled at the discretion of the field commander, particularly as such cases can be a ruse. The Chinese command was further to blame because when Nanking was recognized to be indefensible, it could have been declared an open city.

Deaths apart from these categories are claimed not to have exceeded the scale inevitable in the capture of a major city. None of the various total figures give any breakdown among categories or circumstances. An intent to commit genocide is denied in the light of Japanese history where, although wars have been ruthlessly fought, there are claimed to be no records of massacre for its own sake. This is contrasted with cases of genocide in other countries, such as that committed by the ancient Israelites on the Canaanites, the Mongols in their initial penetration of China, the Spanish and Portuguese extermination of heretics, the French extermination of the natives of Martinique, and that by the British in Tasmania. This last case is described as having been a substitute for hunting, of which the English are notoriously fond, since Koalas are not a satisfactory quarry and no other alternative was available.

Most recent was the Nazi holocaust of the Jews, which the speakers claim was the sole real reason for the Nuremberg trials. This was also the reason why the category 'crimes against humanity' was created in the sense of being committed on some collective group of victims, rather than individuals. Following from this, when the Tokyo Trials were held as an inappropriate imitation of Nuremberg (of which more later) the Nanking massacre was fabricated as an equivalent to the Holocaust. Its 'star witness' at the Tokyo Trial, Father Magee, when questioned by the American defense attorney Captain Brooks as to how many murders he had witnessed replied that there was only one. The rest, the speakers claim, was hearsay or fabrication. The expression 'disposal' occurring in military records need not imply death but may only refer to disarming, release, or evacuation.

The speakers, in conclusion, list the following claimed results of research by Tanaka in his *Overview*. Their scope is restricted to the walled city itself which would of course involve lower figures than the more extended scope adopted by Honda and most others.

1. Although total deaths are alleged to exceed 300,000, no such numbers were present in the city. Documents from the International Committee controlling the Safety Zone give a population of 200,000, the U.S. magazine *Life* 150,000, and records by captured Chinese officers 100,000 to 200,000, to which was added a defending force of 50,000.

2. International Committee documents indicate an increase in city population after Japanese occupation, which is inconsistent with the Tokyo Trials account of six weeks of massacre, assault, and pillage. Research by Dr L.S.C. Smythe, professor of sociology at Chinling University, carried out at the end of March 1938, indicate a population of 221,150. He also notes a possible 250,000—270,000 total if including transients.

3. Despite testimony at the Trials of piles of corpses everywhere, none of the hundred or more Japanese news reporters and cameramen who entered the city with the troops witnessed such sights, nor did foreigners, who included the 15 members of the International Committee and five journalists.

4. The International Committee protested to the Japanese authorities on 425 cases of misconduct. Its secretary, Dr Smythe, recognized that not all were corroborated and discrepancies are reported by Fukuda Atsuyasu (later a Diet member) who handled them. Total murders, even if all true, came to 49.

5. Noncombatants including resident women and children were all living in the Safety Zone. Its German chairman Rabe addressed a letter of thanks to the Japanese command for refraining from shelling the zone and arranging for consultation on aid for Chinese civilians there. On New Year's day 1938, the branch of the Red Swastika Society [Buddhist equivalent of the Red Cross]

also sent a letter of acknowledgment and thanks for supplies to other refugee zones around the city.

6. A 1984 article in the *Asahi Journal* on the massacre, based on an interview with a former NCO, gave a figure of 13,000 killed to his knowledge but the interviewee later claimed distortion as he had actually said that, of 14,000 prisoners taken, half were released. Then, in disorder from a fire next day, half the rest escaped. The other victims were shot in the course of rioting during their transfer.

7. In the Tokyo Trials judgment, a total of 200,000 killed was said to be based on a figure of 155,000 corpses buried by burial teams and other organizations, against which the defense argued that these figures had been compiled ten years after the event and judging by their locations would mainly be battle dead. Then in 1985, Ara Ken'ichi discovered that the Ch'ungshant'ang benevolent institution, which had been recorded as burying 110,000, had not been conducting funerals and burials at the time and was on record as having resumed these only in September 1938.

8. After the dissolution of the International Committee, Dr Smythe obtained the cooperation of students to investigate casualties in and adjoining the walled city. These took a sampling of one in 50 households for direct inquiry and arrived at a result of 850 deaths from military action, 2,400 deaths from violence by troops, and 4,200 abducted or missing.

9. Nationalist War Minister General Ho Ying-ch'in reported on the fall of Nanking to a plenary session of the Provisional National Assembly in spring 1938, and although detailed statistics were appended to other aspects, there was no report on a massacre by the Japanese army.

10. The first mention of the battle of Nanking in the Chinese Communist Party's *War Bulletin* appears in June 1938, but there is no mention of a massacre of civilians or prisoners. The contemporary diary of Agnes Smedley, who accompanied the communist leadership, relates her reflections on the fall of Nanking but mentions no atrocities or massacre. A group of Indian doctors who arrived in Hankow in the summer of 1938 received detailed reports from the Chinese on Japanese crimes and the war situation but no account of a massacre.

11. In the Eighteenth Plenary Session of the League of Nations beginning in August 1937, the Chinese complained about the North China Incident [surrounding the March Polo Bridge clash] and continued to make charges regarding Japanese military operations, so the League passed a resolution condemning Japan [which had left the League some years before]. In 1938, after the fall of Nanking, a resolution in support of China was adopted, with a unanimous condemnation of Japanese bombing and the use of poison gas in Shantung, but there was no charge of a massacre, which did not even appear on the agenda.

12. Japan received frequent protests from the United States, Britain, and France, which had numerous interests in China, including a joint protest on

the indiscriminate bombing of Nanking. Smythe estimated about 600 deaths due to bombing, but there was no protest about a massacre.

Under point 11, the speakers elsewhere suggest that the nationalists' failure to declare Nanking an open city or formally surrender it deprived them of good grounds for complaining of a massacre, though this to some extent undermines their argument that Chinese silence indicates the absence of such an event. In conclusion, however, they claim that these arguments against the truth of the massacre have been so effective that it was not mentioned even in the Diet's humiliating Fiftieth Anniversary Resolution.

Refuting the Tokyo Trial view

As discussed earlier, both the legal basis and the procedure of the Tokyo Trials can and have been criticized on quite objective grounds in both Japan and abroad. Among the judges themselves, six delivered dissenting judgments in whole or in part. The speakers in the present study quote General MacArthur himself, after his dismissal in 1951, as telling President Truman that the trials were a mistake and would serve no purpose for preventing future wars. Justice Douglas of the U.S. Supreme Court, as well as other Western jurists, are quoted as supporting Justice Pal's rejection of *ex post facto* legislation. Although this criticism does not apply to B and C class trials in court-martial form, the speakers also dismiss these as 'revenge trials' or 'victor's justice.'

Unlike some other types of critics of the trials, they do not attack their politically or otherwise selective nature, such as the immunity granted the Emperor, the exclusion of most civilian leaders, and the omission of Unit 731, as well as the arbitrary abandonment of the trials for Cold War purposes. This is because they regard the trials as still essentially designed to criminalize the whole Japanese nation, though in fact, as has been noted, part of the purpose was to narrow blame as far as possible to military leadership. It is noteworthy that the present speakers do not raise the question of the Emperor's war responsibility, which is such a sore issue to the hard-core right wing, merely quoting his Monologue to the effect that the war was over racial discrimination and oil. Unit 731 does not seem to leave any room for debate, unlike Nanking.

The speakers in any case are essentially concerned with the trials' legal basis and in this respect add some distinctive points. Before the postwar framing of the war crimes charter defining 'crimes against peace' and 'against humanity,' the principle of national sovereignty had meant that 'reasons of state' were not subject to any external restriction. This, they claim, arose from the traditional Christian distinction between private and state morality. In the former case, Christians are enjoined to 'love their enemies' on the personal level, but on the national level, such devout Christians as Otto the Great, first Holy Roman Emperor, and Alfred the Great of England prosecuted all-out war on heathen Slavs and Danes with the Pope's blessing. 'Only through confusion of private morality and reason of state could government executives be held individually liable for acts of state.'

Supporters of the trials, they recognize, attempt to find an earlier basis for overriding reasons of state in the 1927 resolution passed by the League of Nations condemning aggressive war and the 1928 Kellogg-Briand Pact renouncing war as a means of settling international disputes, but these documents, they point out, did not refer to any penalty for infringement or to criminal liability for individuals. Regarding the nature of aggression, the Nuremberg definition in terms of 'infringement of treaties, agreements or guarantees' is not exhaustive and the United Nations Charter Article 42 leaves it to the Security Council to define and oppose aggressive war on an ad hoc basis, which would be subject to the national interests of Council members.

The Tokyo Trials treated Japan's aggression as beginning with Manchuria in 1931 but, although the League of Nations adopted a resolution calling on Japan to withdraw troops to the railway zone, which they were permitted to garrison under earlier agreements, Japan was not declared an aggressor, with the application of sanctions, as Italy was in 1935 for the invasion of Ethiopia. In 1939, too, the Soviet Union was expelled from the League for attacking Finland. The United States, which had never joined the League because of isolationist opposition, merely issued a warning to Japan in terms of the 1922 'status quo' Washington Pact and the Kellogg-Briand Pact. Although the Lytton Report to the League was the basis of its resolution for troop withdrawal, the tone of the report was restrained because Britain and France were apprehensive about their own territorial holdings and interests in China, which were on the same legal basis as Japan's under the Unequal Treaties. There was no question of a call for Japan's expulsion from the League, and the speakers condemn the then government for withdrawing from the League unnecessarily.

Returning to trial procedure, they reject the charge of a coherent 'conspiracy' on the grounds that, though meaningful in the German case in view of monolithic Nazi control there, it was applied quite incongruously to Japan—a procedure 'as grotesque as grafting a gorilla's head on a human body.' In contrast with Nazism's iron grip and consistency of purpose, in Japan's case there was no such continuity, as demonstrated by the 12 changes of cabinet between the Manchurian Incident and the Pacific War, nor any reasoned coherent objective. So the idea of an overall conspiracy is nonsense. In the words of one of the class A accused, General Araki Sadao, a prewar War Minister and leader of the anti-Tojo Imperial Way faction in the Army: 'how could I have been in a conspiracy with people whom I had never met or even seen?'

In regard to the death sentences which resulted, the speakers reverse the widespread view, shared by Justice Roeling, that the sole civilian executed, Hirota, did not merit this sentence, in contrast to the military figures executed.

In their view, he was the only one who merited it because members of the armed forces were merely doing their duty as determined by national policy. Hirota, on the other hand, had more responsibility for policy. This was not for his role as prime minister, for which he was mainly condemned, but for his later role as foreign minister in breaking off attempts to negotiate with the Chinese Nationalist government when resistance continued after the fall of Nanking. Negotiations were still possible, since Chiang Kai-shek spoke of Japan being 'an external wound while the Communists were a deep-seated internal disease.' The abandonment of negotiations led to Japan's being mired in the China war and eventually Pearl Harbor. The speakers even claim that, if Japan had been free of the China war, it would not have been defeated in a conflict with the United States—a characteristic hypothetical scenario of the kind appearing in Komuro's *This is how the Pacific War could have been Won*.

On the other hand, execution is particularly deplored in the case of general Matsui, commander at Nanking, as not appropriate for the purely negative crime of non-feasance in failure to prevent the 'alleged massacre.' No evidence for an order actively directing a massacre had been produced.

Other wartime issues and Japanese policy failings

Reasonably enough, the speakers locate Japan's military involvements from the 1930s as arising in a context created by centuries of Western penetration going back to the Portuguese and Spanish. Japanese participation in the Unequal Treaty System already established by the Western powers in China, which Japan achieved through the war of 1894, meant that Japanese garrisons in Manchuria and elsewhere shared the same legal status as British, American, French, and Portuguese garrisons stationed in their respective territories and concessions. This was also similar, they point out, to the stationing of U.S. forces in Japan and South Korea at present, and they go on to claim that the contemporary weakness of Japanese politicians in relation to China arises from a mistaken view of the nature of the war in China.

Even the Tokyo Trials, they argue, did not deny that fighting began in July 1937 with shots being fired at Japanese troops carrying out training maneuvers, but this is claimed to have been triggered by shooting from Communist agents under Liu Hsiao-ch'i against both Japanese troops and those of the East Hopei Anti-Communist Autonomous government, who then blamed each other. Authorities quoted for this are unspecified writings of Mao Tse-tung, a speech by Liu claiming that the incident at the Marco Polo Bridge ultimately led to the annihilation of both Nationalists and Japanese militarists, and another by the current head of government Chiang Tse-min on the 50th anniversary of the war's end to the effect that 'China led the way to Allied victory by involving Japan in the war.'

Japanese and local Chinese troops openly clashed the next day, but, as both sides harbored suspicions as to who was to blame, an agreement was reached on 11 July for Japanese withdrawal and Chinese suppression of anti-Japanese organizations. Despite this local settlement, however, the respective national governments would not let the matter rest. The Japanese Prime Minister Prince Konoe, under pressure from the War Ministry, dispatched reinforcements to North China supposedly to 'contain the situation,' while a Chinese Nationalist conference at Lushan decided on national resistance. In a clash between these new forces near Tientsin on 28 July, the Japanese mistakenly bombed the barracks of a security unit in T'ungchou belonging to the autonomous regime. The local Japanese commander made a visit of apology to its head, but the security unit, again allegedly with communist incitement, mutinied and massacred 200 Japanese and Korean residents in T'ungchou.

The speakers regret that this episode is omitted from textbook accounts of the war because it was effective in silencing arguments for moderation in Japan. But they also blame Prince Konoe for being swayed by the politically motivated War Ministry rather than the Army General Staff who, as is well known, vigorously opposed expansion of the war because of their accurate assessment of Japan's strategic potential, especially with regard to the Soviet threat. In ignoring their competent advice, the speakers add, Konoe was infringing on the prerogative of supreme command which was properly the sphere of the Emperor. They, however, treat this as a fit matter for 'self-criticism' rather than 'apology' and go on to blame Western and Soviet support for Chinese resistance, in their own interests, as having prolonged the war when a settlement might otherwise have been possible. They especially single out the U.S. China lobby centered on Chiang Kai-shek's wife and the politicized missionary community.

In 1940, Wang Ching-wei, a top Nationalist leader after failing to convince Chiang Kai-shek that continued war with Japan could only end in a Communist victory, came over to Japan and established the client Nanking regime, staffed by like-minded elements. The speakers claim that if his policy had been successful and Communism defeated, China would have been spared the reported tens of millions of deaths arising from the Cultural Revolution and other disastrous results of the Communist regime which, they imply, far exceeded the casualties suffered in the war with Japan (possibly true by some estimates).

Their treatment of the oil embargo and the ABCD encirclement follow the usual lines but introduces the claim that it would have been possible to overcome this threat by seizing Indonesia without involving the U.S. Isolationism was still strong there, and President Roosevelt had promised in his last election campaign never to lead the country into war. They claim, interestingly enough, that 'unlike Japanese politicians, those of the United States cannot break election promises.' Japan's membership of the Axis alliance, they admit, made such a course less feasible, and this alliance is seen as another mistake by Prince Konoe in his second spell as prime minister in 1940. He is described as having concluded it as a result of Japanese losses in border clashes with the Soviet Union (actually not the main factor), though the speakers claim that documents now available from the former Soviet Union indicate that the Japanese forces were not worsted as badly as previously thought.

A last major criticism is directed to Japan's reaction to the Hull Note, received from U.S. Secretary of State Cordell Hull on 26 November 1941 after months of tense negotiations and demanding Japanese withdrawal from all external territories and abandonment of the Axis alliance. The speakers claim that the Japanese government, in then breaking off negotiations, had mistaken the Note's intent because it mentioned no deadline and was therefore not an ultimatum. They interpret this as a sign that it was a maximum negotiating position and full compliance was not seriously expected.

Finally, they claim that Foreign Ministry staff, who bungled the transmission of Japan's Final Note until after the attack on Pearl Harbor had begun, deserved the death penalty for bringing such disgrace on Japan (the Emperor's characteristic regret at this breach of protocol is well-known).

Japanese colonialism and Korean questions

The treatment of Japanese colonialism in Korea follows a similar pattern of partial justification and partial criticism of Japanese policies. The speakers begin by claiming that the Korean War of the 1950s made Americans understand for the first time that Japan's intervention in Korea at the beginning of the century was justified to avert the danger presented by a hostile power (Russia or Russian backed) controlling that highly strategic peninsula.

They support the recent statement by former Foreign Minister Watanabe Michio that the treaty of annexation was completed amicably, adding further explanation that the monarchs of both countries were afraid of a Russian war of revenge after the 1905 defeat by Japan and agreed that the union of both countries was necessary to counter such a threat. None of the powers challenged the legality of the annexation. That it did not involve racial discrimination is claimed to be demonstrated by the marriage of the Korean Crown Prince to a Japanese imperial princess (which in fact was used to promote a policy of intermarriage but with the ultimate aim of eliminating Korean national identity).

Komuro here criticized the Japanese policy of displacing the Korean royal house, particularly since Japan claimed to have fought the wars with China and Russia to preserve Korea's independence from both powers. He argued that, since Korea through most of its history had been tributary to China, dating by Chinese emperors' reigns and sending regular tribute missions, the Koreans would have accepted a tributary relationship to Japan more readily than annexation. Once annexation was decided, however, if the Koreans had been

130

given equal franchise under the 1889 Constitution, the two countries might have achieved a successful relationship like that between England and Scotland. But his interlocutor Watanabe doubted that, as Japan had made so much of freeing Korea from its tributary status to China, its people would have been willing to return to such a status.

Both agreed, however, that Japanese rule brought benefits to Korea, such as providing the infrastructure for a modern economy and for the first time introducing basic education to the illiterate mass of the people (though in fact the use of Korean in education was later replaced by Japanese). They note that Japan did not inflict on Korea any disaster of the magnitude of the Irish famine of 150 years ago under British rule and deny that the Koreans were forced to adopt Japanese names (though in fact three-quarters did so under various forms of pressure).

Regarding the frequent current friction between Japan and both Korean regimes, they deprecate the efforts of Japanese politicians to placate them because the mutual hostility between both of those regimes makes proper accord with either of them impossible at present. They point out that Germany only remained divided as long as rivalry between the western and eastern blocs prevented unification, which was achieved smoothly when the Cold War ended. But the end of the Cold War had no such effect in Korea, so Japan should not court the Koreans so assiduously until they compose their own differences.

South Korean claims to be fearful of future Japanese aggression are seen to be hollow from the absence of any fortifications at Pusan—all defensive measures being directed northward only. In any case, under existing world conditions, classic imperialism is not a viable undertaking anywhere. Japan should not entertain individual claims for war compensation being advanced by Koreans or others, as all of Japan's postwar obligations by treaty have been fulfilled. Such claims were encouraged by Prime Minister Hosokawa's acceptance of the charge of 'aggression.' Watanabe remarks that, although Hosokawa was a graduate of his own university of Sophia, he was subsequently employed by the *Asahi* and absorbed the '*Asahi* view of history.'

Japan's ultimate triumph

The symposium concludes with the speakers recounting successes that Japanese can view with satisfaction. Japan's economic achievements in the half century since saturation bombing, including atomic bombs, has inspired other countries to follow its example. Although Japan was defeated in its own ambitions for colonial empire, it was the Western colonial powers that suffered the greatest setbacks. Many of the peoples liberated by the retreat of imperialism were able to use both the Japanese model and Japanese aid to compete with the West themselves. Next, the other great challenge for world domination presented by the Communist sphere ended with the collapse of the East European bloc and the Soviet Union itself, as well as China's shift to a market economy. Both processes closed the four-century hegemony of the white race. 'Although this may be described as a right wing view of history,' it agrees with the judgment of P. F. Drucker in *The New Realities* (1989) that Japanese economic development was a most important factor in preserving world freedom. When the Eastern European countries saw their own economic success falling far behind that of former colonies in East and Southeast Asia, they were convinced of the failure of their own system. Japan therefore ultimately achieved the true aims of the Greater East Asia War. First has been its continued security, the stated aim in the Rescript declaring War. Second is the achievement of a free trade order, overcoming such barriers as economic blocs, of the kind arising from the Great Depression, and the ABCD embargo. Third, although not mentioned directly in the Rescript but a tacit corollary of it, was the liberation of the colonial areas and the prosperity of those areas where Japanese influence was strongest, namely South Korea, Taiwan, and Southeast Asia, 'except the Philippines where, as in Latin America, U.S. influence has not been so beneficial.'

Whatever the possible merit of any of the particular points raised in the symposium, this sample of revisionist argument is probably adequate to explain how ideological ammunition of this kind can impart to figures of neonationalist persuasion the confidence to advance such views in public or on the level of point-scoring in debate. In education, as noted earlier, the textbook screening system now tends to curb the more extreme of such views and rather to favor accounts of the war congenial to mainly Asian societies who desire proof that Japan has renounced its militaristic past, but the possibility remains that this combination of conditions may merely result in a widespread tendency to an Orwellian double-think. Again, the future of the constitutional debate should provide the best index of the public mind.

A final word

Scattered media reports of Nanking denial or textbook censorship give a simplistically hostile picture of Japanese officials and government. In fact, the full story is complicated, and a fair share of the blame lies beyond Japan's shores. Churchill's insistence at the onset of the Cold War that 'our policy should be to draw the sponge across the crimes and horrors of the past ... and look towards the future' was a powerful invitation to amnesia while the personal backing of U.S. presidents of such reactionaries as Kishi and Nakasone served only to abet distortion and revisionism.

Japan's wartime amnesia has to be seen in the powerful context of the Cold War and 'reverse course,' neither of which were of her making. Nevertheless, with the Cold War now in the past, Japan must accept more responsibility for its future. Ienaga Saburo and his associates as the conscience of Japan will be watching and waiting.

Select annotated bibliography

The basic sources used in this book are noted in this bibliography. In cases where substantial amounts have been quoted, attribution is made in the text. Where thought desirable, titles are briefly annotated.

Bix, Herbert P. 1992. 'The Showa Emperor's Monologue and the Problem of War Responsibility,' *The Journal of Japanese Studies* 18, 2:295-363.

Bungei Shunju Co (ed.) 1995. *Nihonjin no Hatsugen: Sengo 50-nen* (The Japanese Utterance: 50 years after the War) (2 vols.). Tokyo. A comprehensive collection of major 'utterances' prominent in public life over the period mentioned.

Buruma, Ian 1994. *The Wages of Guilt: Memories of War in Germany and Japan.* Jonathan Cape, London.

Fujiwara, Akira (ed.) 1988. *Senso no Shinjitsu o Jugyo ni* (The Truth of the War in Lessons). Ayumi Shuppan, Tokyo. Outlines of major wartime issues by various specialists and studies on the method of teaching about them.

Harris, Sheldon H. 1994. *Factories of Death: Japanese Biological Warfare 1932-45 and the American Cover-up.* Routledge, London.

Hicks, George 1995. *The Comfort Women: Sex Slaves of the Japanese Imperial Forces.* Allen and Unwin, St. Leonards, Australia.

Honda, Katsuichi 1983. *Hinkon naru Seishin: Dai 14 shu* (An impoverished Spirit: Collection 14). Suzusawa Shoten, Tokyo.

_____ 1991. *Hinkon naru Seishin: G-shu* (An impoverished Spirit: Collection G). Asahi Shimbunsha, Tokyo.

Ienaga, Saburo (trans Baldwin, F.) 1978. *The Pacific War 1931-45: A Critical Perspective on Japan's Role in World War 11.* Random House, New York.

_____ 1995. *Watashi ga omou koto* (What I think). Minshusha, Tokyo. A collection of columns from Ienaga's support group's *Textbook Suit News.*

Irokawa, Daikichi (ed.) 1995. *Haisen kara Nani o mananda ka: Nihon, Doitsu, Itaria* (What was learned from Defeat? Japan, Germany, Italy). Shogakkan, Tokyo. Comparative studies of postwar attitudes.

Ishida, Osamu 1995. *Shimbun ga Nihon o dame ni shita* (The Newspapers ruined Japan). Gendai Shorin, Tokyo. Their prewar, wartime, and postwar roles.

Itoh, Mayumi 1995. 'Japanese Politician's "Attitudinal Prism:" Racial Superiority Complex towards Asia.' Paper for the Seventh Annual Meeting of the Far West Popular Culture and American Culture Associations, Las Vegas, USA.

Johnson, Chalmers 1995. *Japan: Who Governs?* W.W. Norton, New York.

Komuro Naoki and Watanabe Shoichi 1995. *Fuin no Showa-shi* (Showa History under Seal). Tokuma Shoten, Tokyo. A neonationalistic symposium.

Kusaka Kimindo and Komuro Naoki 1995. *Taiheiyo Senso ko sureba kateta* (This is how the Pacific War could have been won). Kodansha, Tokyo. An example of alternative hypothetical scenarios on the war.

Kyokasho Kentei Sosho wo Shien-suru Tokyo-to Renrakukai (Tokyo Prefecture Liaison Council for Support of the School Textbook Screening Suit) (ed.) 1995. *Ajia kara mita Nihon no Kyokasho Mondai* (The Japanese Textbook Issue viewed from Asia). Kamogawa Shuppan, Kyoto.

Kyokasho Kentei Sosho o shien-suru Zenkoku Renrakukai (National League for Support of the School Textbook Screening Suit) 1994. *Ima Taisetsu naru mono wa Kodomo, Inochi, Mirai* (The Important things now are children, Life and the Future). Tokyo. Detailed material on the third lawsuit.

Large, Stephen S. 1992. *Emperor Hirohito and Showa Japan.* Routledge, London.

McGregor, Richard 1996. *Japan Swings.* Allen and Unwin, St. Leonards, Australia.

Nik-kan Rekishi Kyokasho Kenkyukai (Japan-South Korea History Textbook Research association) (ed.) 1993. *Kyokasho o Nik-kan Kyoryoku de kangaeru* (Studying Textbooks with Japanese-South Korean Cooperation). Otsuki Shoten, Tokyo.

Ota, Takashi 1994. *Watashi to Ienaga Kyokasho Saiban* (The Ienaga Textbook Case and Myself). Hitotsubashi Shobo, Tokyo.

Rekishi Kyoikusha Kyogikai (Council of History Educators) 1995. *Sengo-shi kara Nani o Manabu ka?* (What is to be learned from Postwar History?). Aoki Shoten, Tokyo.

Shida Ichiro 1989. *Chosen no Rekishi to Nihon* (Korea's History and Japan). Akashi Shoten, Tokyo.

Takashima, Nobuyoshi 1994. *Kyokasho wa ko kakinaosareta* (How Textbooks have been Re-written). Kodansha, Tokyo. Problems and progress in textbook developments, by the plaintiff in the Yokohama lawsuit.

Tawara Yoshifumi and Ishiyama Hisao 1995. *Kyokasho Kentei to Konnichi no Kyokasho Mondai no Shoten* (Textbook screening and the Focus of Today's Textbook Issue). Gakushunotomo Sha, Tokyo.

Williams, Peter and Wallace, David 1989. *Unit 731.* Grafton Books, London.

Yoshida, Yutaka 1995. *Nihonjin no Senso-kan* (Japanese Views of the War). Iwanami Shoten, Tokyo. An overview of the whole postwar period.

Periodicals

Recent numbers of the following periodicals have been consulted:

Kyokasho Saiban Nyusu (Textbook Suit News). Tokyo. Published monthly by the National League for Support of the School Textbook Screening Suit.
Kyokasho Reporto (Textbook Report). Published yearly by the Federation of Publishing Employees Unions, Tokyo.